If You Were There, You'd Know

If You Were There, You'd Know

Published by North of Faith Publications, 2024

stevekemsley.com
steve@stevekemsley.com

ISBN: 978-1-0685115-3-0
eBook ISBN: 978-1-0685115-2-3

Copyright © Steve Kemsley, 2024

Typeset by The Book Typesetters
thebooktypesetters.com

If You Were There, You'd Know – Wham!

A Memoir

by

Steve Kemsley

Start Me Up

What on earth are you writing a book for? Who gives a fuck about your life? Why? These are just some of the comments I have received when mentioning that I fancied writing down some memories. "Who are you writing it for?" asked my partner, Sasha. The answer is simple. I'm writing it for me… if no one reads it, I'm not sure if I will really care; however, I do think those that matter the most to me will probably read it, although I am thinking about a redacted version for my children and parents.

To my mind, my life has been quite a journey and as is the case in everyone's life, there are always lessons to be learnt, stories and moments that I think are worth telling. I've had a 40-year career in what some might describe as media, others would say entertainment with a fair sprinkling of show business. As far as I'm concerned, my life has been bloody fantastic.

I'm not going to write with floweriness nor use words that I don't understand. Instead, I'm going to try and tell you how it was from my perspective, in plain English. I've listened to a lot of autobiographies recently and sometimes the authors try too hard to create poetic phrases using fancy English. That frustrates me, so forgive me if I'm direct. I like brevity; "less is more" is a life mantra for me.

"When I was younger, so much younger than today," I wanted to be a famous DJ, but I certainly have no desire to be famous now, quite unlike my now somewhat-famous brother, PK. He enjoys fame, in fact, if he likes this book, maybe I'll write his biography. I can assure you his story will be more of a rollercoaster than some of mine, but that's subjective. I've had some crazy stuff happen in my life, sad days, traumatic days, but the majority of my days have been happy. Many people seem to think this writing process will be a cathartic experience, I'm not finding it cathartic so far. I'm just enjoying the process of writing and keeping my mind engaged soon after selling my third business. Creativity has been front and centre in my life and this attempt at writing a book I see as a challenge that I relish. I hope you enjoy reading it as much as I've enjoyed writing it. I decided to name both the book and all the chapters after songs by some of my favourite artists, for reasons you'll get along the way....

Chapter 1

When it Started to Begin

Nick Heyward

'm really proud I was born a true Londoner, 20th July, 1965 in the Middlesex Hospital, Goodge Street just off of the Tottenham Court Road. Mum was young, only 21 years old and Dad had begun life as a chartered accountant and was six years older (still is). Many years later, my last West End production office was situated at the top of Newman Street approximately 150 yards from the site where it all began for me.

I was the first of three boys for Mum and Dad; Paul (PK) came next, two years later, and Andrew a further two years after that, but much more about them later!

We lived in a suburb of London called Stanmore – it's

at the very end of the Jubilee line today; it was the Metropolitan line back then. Life seemed pretty normal to us, it was what one might described as a typical middle-class upbringing with Dad being a professional, and we didn't seem to go without. Playtime was outdoors, we lived with our neighbours and cousins being our closest friends and we rode our bikes – I had a Chopper, PK a Chipper and Andrew probably a much smaller affair. We kicked footballs and got along great although with Andrew being four years younger than me, I'm not sure I had too much to do with him in those early years. Talking to friends' parents later in life, it seems Mum was (and still is) fastidiously clean and tidy, apparently she had us all in bed by 6pm every night with the house all *shpigl* (a Yiddish word for 'clean and tidy'), for Dad to come home to I guess. When their friends came to dinner, there was apparently no evidence that three children lived there at all.

We were a Jewish family but not really practising; Dad moved to Reform Jewry from the more Orthodox because he wanted to sit next to Mum if we ever went to *shul* (synagogue), a great reason. We went to Hebrew school and all got Barmitzvah'd, but we were never as observant as our cousins. Once I had children of my own, I actually had a period where

I enjoyed going to shul just before my boys' Barmitzvahs but that was fairly short-lived and as I type today, I'm pretty agnostic about religion. I do love being a Jew and I'm proud to be one. I've enjoyed many visits to Israel over the years and I have friends and family that live there. I think I'm a spiritual person who believes in the universe as opposed to God, but I do love the cultural side of being a Jew… the togetherness, the community, the sense of being and of course the food!

We lived in two houses in Stanmore. My first-ever home was in Pangbourne Drive and then before Andrew came along we were in a nice mock-Georgian detached home in Georgian Close. This is where my earliest memories emanate from; this is where we dressed up as Cowboys and Indians, played on the climbing frame in a nice-sized back garden and made good friends with the neighbours. My very first memory was playing with Stickle Bricks waiting for baby Andrew to arrive home;

There isn't much to say about my younger childhood as all my recollections are standard boring ones. Life just carried on as I imagine it did in most homes in our community in those days. I feel like life began in earnest when we moved further out to Hatch End in

Middlesex another four or so miles west and I was about ten years old. We moved schools too and that seemed a big deal.

My first school was Stanburn in Stanmore and I had a couple of good friends there, one called Milton (who I still know today) and another called Stephen. We knocked about as best mates do between the ages of five and ten years old. I remember the smell of freshly cut grass on the first day we were allowed to play on the 'field' at school. We used to line up, the whole school, waiting for the teacher to say the grass was dry enough and if it was, the whole school would cheer, scream and run to the top of the field and back again, sitting down to make daisy chains. How exciting... it's the small things...

My only other memory from Stanburn was a gymnastics display I had to do, where I got to pick the music I performed the routine to. Mum had a Neil Diamond cassette and I thought the song *A Beautiful Noise* was brilliant and used it – this must have been my first true encounter with pop music around 1975 when I was ten.

Pop music has fuelled my life ever since. *Top of the Pops* was an absolute must every Thursday. What a tragedy it was when it came off-air along with *The Tube*, two staples of my musical upbringing that were crucial to me and so brilliant to have had in the mainstream of British TV culture during the formative years of my life.

Chapter 2

Home
Michael Bublé

So there we were, all five of us in a pretty fancy brand new house at the bottom of Royston Park Road in Hatch End. None of my friends lived this far out, so new friends had to be made and there was a new school called Grimsdyke. I didn't like school; I didn't hate it, but it was what it was and I was the last boy in the school still wearing short trousers… Mum! Why? I got bullied, I don't remember feeling weak or inferior but I guess in every school there were the bullies and those who got bullied. One day, my tormentor, who I think was called Simon, lay in wait over the bridge on my way home and he had a bunch of stinging nettles in his hand which was protected by his pulled-down jumper sleeve and he just wiped them over my exposed legs. What a cunt! I ran home crying and was in long trousers from then on. Again, I have no remarkable memory from this school, just nothing. I went back there once, later in life, and can only remember thinking how small everything was and how it still smelt of sick.

So my memories seem to begin from about the age of 12. I'm not sure why I don't recall much before this age. I'm inclined to think it's because nothing remarkable happened. A few years ago, I found myself in therapy after the break-up of my marriage and my therapist kept hinting that there must be reasons why I don't recall much about these years. I did try, but 'zip', as they say.

Our house was cool; the main internal wall was exposed brickwork and we had open-tread stairs, all very trendy back then. Dad seemed to work hard, coming home close to our bedtime, and Mum made us tea every night. I remember Mum and Dad had a stack Hi-Fi stereo system in the posh lounge, which always smelt a little stale as it was hardly ever used, and I used to make cassettes of the charts in there every Sunday afternoon. I didn't have a record player yet, but I was soon to be 13 and my Barmitzvah was close. I had extra Hebrew lessons so I would know my 'portion' and the blessings off by heart come the big day. What a weird process – a deeply religious tradition that you just learnt by heart. By far the best thing and the reason so many study for this day was the inevitable gifts that were going to come my way – it's a kind of a means to an end. The gifts didn't disappoint. I got money (which a couple of years later I used to buy my first mobile disco). I got a cool '70s initial signet ring which my daughter, Saskia, still wears today, but most importantly I got a record player from my Papa Issy's second wife who we called Auntie Anne. Wow, it was a white, plastic, rubbish, cheap thing from Boots, but I loved it, it worked and now I could buy records!

My first real musical memories were a few years earlier. One of our grandfathers, Papa Issy (the nicest, kindest, sweetest human I have ever known) used to drive us in his big Daimler with leather seats and he had an 8-track cassette player in there... I loved listening to Max Bygraves and the soundtrack to *Oliver! The Musical*, learning all the words to great songs like *I'm a Pink Toothbrush, You're a Blue Toothbrush* and *I'd Do Anything*.

I was lucky enough to have another Papa and Grandma – my Dad's parents. Grandma Betty was quite unique, she showered me with kisses and love when we met, but that wasn't often as they lived in Bournemouth. Papa Harry was a quiet, simple man, a proper cockney cabinet maker from the East End of London, happily retired, but Grandma ruled the roost. It's easy to reflect as an adult now, but Grandma Betty was a bit mean and always thought she'd married beneath her station, not that she was anything posh or special. She said silly stuff and changed her accent to a posher one whenever she could. "Oh, have you met my son, Kenny? He's a chartered accountant, you know." "Have you just come back from your villa in Spain, son?" Her audience for this soliloquy was a carer in an old age home who didn't speak much English. She was from the East End as well, so not very posh at all, but she would wear her mink coat whenever she could.

I'll never forget staying with them in Bournemouth once and Papa shaking the ketchup to make me laugh, forgetting to put the lid on, which resulted in a huge splurge of red sauce on the ceiling. Grandma went mad at him and I thought it was hysterical. It was the late 70s and I was allowed to stay up a lot later at theirs than at home. One night, there was a programme on called *Bouquet of Barbed Wire*. It was the first time I'd seen naked breasts on television. Grandma went pink and said she thought I shouldn't be watching this and "Wasn't it time for bed?" Funny what you remember, but tits are memorable for a young boy!

Now 13, how was I going to get any regular money to buy records? Dad gave us fuck all pocket money and whatever we got all disappeared on 'tuck'. He was always encouraging us to find our own way in life, some might say he was tight, Mum says frugal or careful, but my view today is that I couldn't want to learn a better discipline in life than earning my own money which ultimately helped me craft and control my own destiny.

Car washing was £3 a pop – I used Mum's bucket, washing-up liquid, cloths and sponge. I worked hard and did a least five cars in the street at weekends. Caddying at the golf club was also £3 a round and I spent all my weekends trying to earn some money aged 13 to 15.

At this time, Dad took me up the road to his golf club which was called Grimsdyke (same as my school) and enlisted me to have lessons with the assistant pro, who was called Mark Tibbles. Mark must have been about 19 or 20 and, when you are 14, that's so much older! He had a bit of breakout skin but the fucking coolest hair, long and curly like a rock star and certainly not like a golfer. He was kind, patient and a very good teacher. I'm not sure how or why but we became really friendly. I remember watching the 1980 Olympics at his mum and dad's house in West London, but the biggest influence Mark had on me was his passion for music. He loved a band called Wild Horses and as if by osmosis so then did I. Wild Horses were new and formed by Brian "Robbo" Robertson, the 'wild' Scottish guitarist who played with Thin Lizzy during their heyday of *Live & Dangerous*, the best live album of all time – still to this day in my opinion. I became obsessed quickly and started buying the music press to learn more.

Mark took me to see Wild Horses at the original Marquee Club in Wardour Street more than once. One time, Phil Lynott, Thin Lizzy's lead singer, guested and I thought I was in heaven. Here was a REAL rock star and he was only a few feet away. I could see his sweat, watch it drip off his chin. He was so fucking cool; it was effortless. We all swooned, even the big, fat, hairy rockers. I was only 14 and God knows how Mum and Dad let me out so late on a school night, but this was it – Rock 'n' Roll! I was so small that the metal-heads used to pick me up to get a view, and then I would slide down their sweaty leather jackets. It was so small and hot in that legendary club, but to me it was everything.

I remember coming home late on the train from seeing the gig, and when in my bedroom setting my clock radio alarm for school, my ears were ringing so much from the gig that apparently I had the radio on so loud that I woke up Dad, who came in and asked what I was doing. "Sorry," I said sheepishly and omitted to tell him that the reason why the radio was blasting was because I'd been deafened by a heavy rock show in the West End. I reckon I'd told them I was going to Mark's house or something. I even had a tour jacket made with the Wild Horses logo on the back; they were a mini obsession.

By now, I had bought my first few records, including the soundtrack to *Grease*, the aforementioned *Live & Dangerous*, Wild Horses' debut album, and quite a few 7" singles. Whatever was in the charts, if I liked it, I bought it. I spent all my money on records, often going without tuck or lunch to buy another single. I wore those records out. I wrote down lyrics longhand in the back of my school exercise books, devoured the sleeve notes, cut out pictures from Sounds, Record Mirror and Melody Maker and started creating my Wild Horses scrapbook. Record

Mirror had a gossip column by Paula Yates and it had a tiny picture of her about the size of a stamp; I fell in love with the girl in the picture (years before she presented *The Tube*) and read it avidly every week. I also started collecting The History of Rock, a once-a-month magazine that I read cover to cover and collected in a big red ring binder. The only reason I mention this now is that many years later, I was asked by De Agostini to make a TV ad for this collection, probably on its 20th reissue; I guess history doesn't change.

Air guitar with a tennis racket was a thing in the privacy of my own bedroom. I had my own room as I was the oldest, and Paul and Andrew had to share. I wanted shaggy hair like Robbo and Mark, so Mum sent me to her best friend who was a hairdresser in Hatch End for a perm. Auntie Pat created a style more like Michael Jackson in The Jackson 5 than Leif Garrett. It was a disaster; I hated it.

Soon after my Barmitzvah, we all went to America for a special holiday. We stayed briefly at the Fontainebleau Hotel in Miami where the waitresses around the pool wore high heels and the skimpiest swimsuits cut down the middle at the front with masses of exposed heavenly flesh. It was the beginning of the 80s; the big hair and the swimsuits was the look in Miami. I didn't know where to look! I needed to calm down with a walk on the beach to the hotel next door where I remember watching the movie *The Champ* starring Jon Voight and Ricky Schroder and crying my eyes out at the emotional scenes, something I still do to this day when watching anything remotely emotional. I'm a very emotional person and cry easily, even at a great vocal or song. When I first heard the mixed recording of George Michael and Queen's live version of *Somebody to Love*, I had to pull the car over and have a cry; it blew me away. I was at that gig but his vocal on the recording was mind-blowing. I digress… I tend to do that a bit.

Back home in Hatch End, I had now landed at another school called Atholl, it was a small private grammar school in Rayners Lane with about 160 pupils – all boys. This was via a short stint at Hatch End High, the local comprehensive, which was rough. I remember being the coolest of the geeks and the weakest of the tough nuts. Hatch End High taught me to wear my tie in a huge triangle, no top button, collar open over my blazer like a 70s hooligan. I remember coming home from that school and shoving my little brothers as I was shoved at school and spitting on the floor, cos that's what they did at school. What horrible short exposure to a rougher side of life that was.

Dad must have started doing ok as I was quickly moved out of the comprehensive and on to this predominately Jewish small private grammar school called Atholl. When I started there, I was determined not to be bullied again, so I went around bashing shoulders with everyone. "What you fucking looking at?" I'd say to these unsuspecting, polite Jewish kids, quickly establishing I wasn't weak, and after a few days of that behaviour I was never bullied again. Ever since those days at Hatch End High, I've always stood up for anyone smaller, weaker, younger or more timid… right up to the present day. I can't stand it when someone is rude to a young waiter or waitress and will always say something to the bully.

So, I'm 13 nearly 14; I was kept down a year at Atholl as a July baby and went from youngest in the year to oldest, and life seemed to be starting. Hormones were beginning to move around and I started flicking through *The ABC of Sex* which I found was on the bookshelf at home. School was still shit but it was against the law not to go.

I was also a Cub and then a Boy Scout; I enjoyed it

all. We were the 16th Edgware and it was fun. I went on my first camping trip with the Scouts where I was made 'camp runner' and given a bar of Ex-Lax on a string to wear around my neck by the bigger boys, the senior Scouts. I had no idea what Ex-Lax was and that night in the comfort of my sleeping bag I opened this tiny cardboard box to discover what appeared to be a small chocolate bar. I ate the lot. FUCK FUCK FUCK, what had I done? A few hours later, in the most basic of latrines, I had the worst diarrhoea of my life. It turns out Ex-Lax was a laxative – camp runner indeed – and one square of the chocolate would have prompted a nice soft bowel movement; the whole bar created the sorest arse in Scouting history.

Something very important in my life occurred at Scouts, apart from learning to light a fire with two sticks. There was this older boy, I must have been 14 or 15 and he was a Venture Scout; he had a brown shirt versus our green ones and he was about 21 years old. One day, he came to Scouts with a gold trinket hanging from a small gold chain over his 'woggle'. "What's that?" I enquired. It looked like a half-opened banana and he explained that he'd just started a mobile disco called Banana Split. Cool, I thought; I wanna do that. He wasn't very cool but had a great personality. He had quite a big nose and

Buggles-like big, thick glasses. Little did either of us know at this point how Julian Posner would later feature in my life in a major way, with a smaller nose and laser-corrected eyes; I perhaps shouldn't mention the now much thicker hair.

Earlier that summer, we, as a family, went to Cyprus with our step-cousins, where I won a disco dancing competition with one of my cousins, Tracey, but what was most notable about this holiday was that it was the first (and one of the only times) I got blind drunk, completely pissed. In those days, they had a thing for new guests called the Manager's Reception, and my brothers and I were due to meet up with Mum and Dad. On the huge catering table at the end of the room, there were rows and rows of cocktails laid out. We were there early and the room was practically empty, so I thought, I was a big boy now; in fact, as far as my religion was concerned, I was a man – I'm gonna try one. Mmmm, that's actually quite nice; it had sugar around the rim of the glass and tasted fruity. I asked what it was and the young waitress said it was a brandy sour. I drank the first one, which was like a tangy fruit juice – no big deal – then the second, maybe even a third. Mum and Dad appeared and we had to go to dinner; our table was across the dance floor in the middle of the dining room, we had the same table every day for all meals. That's when things began to go very wrong.

My world started spinning as I weaved my way unsteadily across this tiny dance floor which seemed to me in this moment as big as a football pitch. I sat down and told my parents that I felt sick. "Go to bed," Dad replied tersely. I think the two-minute journey to my room took me half an hour. I felt awful and was trying not to throw up. I lay down on the marble steps to our first-floor room, momentarily enjoying the cool feel of the marble on my forehead… somehow I made it to my room, lay on the bed, fully clothed with the room whirling like a fairground ride around me. The next day, there were warnings about alcoholic poisoning from Mum and Dad, and thereafter, I didn't touch a drop of alcohol for many years.

Towards the end of that summer, I went to a residential summer school, a sort of 'get the kids out of my hair' place with lots of daily activities and had my first ever proper kiss. I am aware that what I'm about to tell you is a bit shocking, but I need you to know in advance that as far as I was concerned, it was fucking magically amazing. My first snog was with MATRON at summer school! She must have been in her early twenties; it was mind-blowing. In hindsight, she was either being very kind and trying to teach me or she was a dodgy perv. After several secret trysts in her bedroom, she chucked me and went with another geek kid… she must have been a perv. Wow, I was off; from that moment on, I loved girls.

My early successes were limited, but the introduction of local Jewish youth clubs in Pinner and Kenton saw me embark on a four-year-long snog fest, helped greatly by the fact that my record collection was big enough for me to start DJ'ing. I proceeded to kiss so many girls, I would also try and work out what else I could do. *The ABC of Sex* from Mum and Dad's bookshelf was ok, the pencil drawings were informative but rudimentary. I really needed to learn and then one day, as if by magic, I found my first 'girlie' magazine in the bushes by my house; I think it was called Knave, quite brilliant and thrilling. My career in masturbation had begun. I realised that I really did prefer the slightly older lady… must've been matron's fault. All the girls my age just seemed immature to me.

I remember asking my first potential girlfriend on my first ever date. I took the 107 bus from Hatch End to Pinner (for privacy) and using a two pence coin in a phone box, asked Sharon to the movies. She said yes. Brilliant. No, not brilliant. After several nerve-wracking attempts to put my arm around her shoulder in the cinema, maybe trying to hold her hand after, she chucked me the next day because I didn't touch her. I told Sharon this story many years later, she had no reaction apart from a polite smile or any recollection of this seminal (for me) and inaugural date. Oh well….

Back to Atholl school. It was, upon reflection, a strange place, mostly I think because we had a very weird headmaster. Mr Cummings was his name. What a freak! He chain-smoked in school, at assembly, in class and he stunk. He wore one of those long black cloaks and for some reason he took a shine to me. One year, I won the Reading Prize. I was a good orator and thought I had a good voice. I also won the Headmaster's Prize, which proved to be very useful in my final year at Atholl; more about this in a bit…. Mr Stevens was our cool sports teacher; he was nice. I loved sports but was never naturally talented. I did my right knee in at football and then my left knee was shredded on a school skiing trip. It took over 16 weeks to fix my torn ligament which was patched up in Italy and must have torn away from the bone by the time I got home.

There were months of to and fro to Stanmore Orthopaedic Hospital and I was on crutches for three of those months… horrid.

I remember going to school early most days in Year 5 to buy two slices of white toast at the local cafe, just toast and butter – why? Cos there was only fucking brown bread at home and white toast was AMAZING. These were the days of nicking the odd Fruit Salad or Black Jack and if you don't know what these are… well here's a clue, they cost half a pence each; Fruit Salads were chewy pineapple and raspberry flavoured chews and Black Jacks were aniseed and turned your entire mouth black for hours. Daring cat burglar I was never going to be. I'm sure we all remember chewing ours jaws off with Bazooka bubble gum? The taste went within a minute and the cartoons wrapped around the gum were too small to read.

I was friendly with a kid called Sean O'Reilly and his dad Jerry was the chief engineer at London's premier radio station Capital Radio. One day I was invited up to Capital for a look around with Sean, by his dad. It was fantastic for me to see all the studios but on that particular day something even more fantastic happened. Michael Aspel had the mid morning show and his special guest unbeknown to us was

Muhammed Ali. Our visit was timed such that when The Greatest, Ali walked out of the studio we just happened to be in the corridor. I'll never forget offering him my hand when introduced and he pushed it away and said "put 'em up kid" and started feigned boxing us. The scene was totally surreal and we went home with permanent grins and our heads in a spin.

Back to why being the recipient of the Headmaster's Prize turned out to be very useful. I was in the 6th year, O-Level year (now called GCSEs) and at that year's Speech Day, it was announced that I was going to be one of four head boys. Cool, I thought… life goes on, but cool. My regular hangout after school, before getting the 107 bus home, was to hang with a few other boys at 20th Century Cabs just over the hill past Rayners Lane tube station. Here there was a Pac-Man machine and a Space Invaders; we played these games most nights, wasting our 10ps or whatever it cost. They were way more advanced than the Atari tennis game we had at home which was old hat by now.

One such after-school night, one of the cabbies who waited there for their jobs or rides to come in offered our group some hash; sure, I was game. There were four of us, it was £12 for an eighth, £3 each. Problem… I had no money; imagine if I had just left it there… but I didn't. Off I trundled to the nearby Post Office where my savings account had about £15 in it. I withdrew £3, returned to the cab office and partook in this huge drug deal. The next issue was that I had no tobacco or fags, no cigarette papers (skins) and nothing to carry anything in. The cabbie said, "No problem." He proceeded to stuff some tobacco in a 35mm small plastic film canister with some papers and this tiny, tiny bit of hash (we were properly ripped off); it was about half the size of my little fingernail. I stuffed it in my blazer pocket and got the bus home like someone out of *Miami Vice* (not!).

Later that night, I attempted to roll my first ever spliff. I didn't realise I needed to burn the hash; I had no idea how much to put in and ended up with something that resembled a cottonwool bud… I puffed on it out of the quarter-light window in our bathroom, felt nothing, coughed a bit and thought this was all a load of bollocks and a total waste of time and money. (That was two 7" singles I could have purchased.) I put the film case in my top drawer and literally forgot about it. A few days later came what I still think was one of the worst days of my life (I am blessed as I haven't had too many bad days).

Here's the scene – I'm called into the headmaster's office. I knocked nervously. "ENTER!", as Cummings always bellowed, and as I walked in, my Dad was sitting there with another gentleman who I was soon to discover was a police detective. Dad looked stern. "Ah, Kemsley, sit down," said Cummings. I was still clueless as to what this was about. It turns out a podgy, creepy, goody-two-shoes wanker called Anthony Woods had grassed us up for buying the weed. What a cock! Anyway, they were taking this very seriously and gradually our gang of four were all called in. It seems the biggest issue was that they wanted the cabbie who sold us the hash. I honestly didn't know his name and quickly felt that grassing him up was not the best idea. The rest is a bit of a blur, but what I do remember is that after we had described what he vaguely looked like, we were told to go home and not come back that week for fear of retribution. In hindsight, this was all a bit over the top. So Dad drove me home. He was livid. He was so angry he couldn't speak; it was a long, silent drive. It's still to this day as angry as I've ever known my Dad. I was sent straight up to my room, where I handed over the camera film tube with the weed still practically untouched. What then emerged was that my punishment, which could well have been expulsion, was to have my head boy stripes taken from me before they were even sown on my blazer sleeves. I am convinced that I saved the other three boys too as I was Cummings' favourite and, ever since then, as the Electronic song goes, *I've been getting away with it all my life.*

Chapter 3

Music was my First Love

Barry Manilow

Just up the road from my school was the Rayners Lane Record and Disco Centre. I was in that shop every single (get it) day. Two guys ran the shop. They wore real 80s shirts with brightly-coloured jeans and those dicky belts; they both had late 70s beards. I remember one of them was Andy, who gladly took my hard-earned money plus my lunch money in exchange for 7" and 12" singles. I knew by now I wanted to be a DJ, not just for fun; this was a career choice. I was going to be a famous Radio 1 disc jockey. I was obsessed with music, the charts, the fashion and the whole scene. I devoured the music press. I saw ads for gigs and needed to start going to them. So, in my lunch hour, I would take the tube to Hammersmith and buy tickets to gigs at the legendary Hammersmith Odeon (now the Apollo) – Haircut 100, ABC, Wham!, Duran Duran; they all played there, and I simply had to be there.

During this period, I got a job at Wembley Market with a client of my Dad's accountancy practice. He sold car seat covers! I had to get the first train from Hatch End to Wembley at about 5 am on freezing cold Sunday mornings. I worked hard, got paid about £15 and on the way home, walked past The Empire Pool – Wembley, where I often spent my cash buying four tickets to Supertramp or Wings, selling two of them for double what they cost and therefore making my tickets free. These Wembley shows were actually amongst the first I attended, aged about 15. Concerts were incredible; I loved them then as I still do today.

During my life, I have seen thousands of gigs since that early Wild Horses show at the Marquee on Wardour Street. Incredible shows by incredible acts. I went to Live Aid in '85 and Wham! The Final, both at Wembley Stadium. I'm thinking about listing as many of them as I can remember but it may be easier to list the bands I haven't seen.

We saw U2 in New York later in Boston and in 2024 at The Sphere in Las Vegas, The Police in New York at Madison Square Garden, The Stones in Spielberg, Austria, Jamie Callum in Majorca. These are just a few of the international gig jaunts. There was one time where I had insane platform tickets at Wembley Stadium for a Michael Jackson show, we got walked through the crowd with the VIPs and everyone looked and wondered who we were.

I promised myself at that young age that I would go to as many gigs as possible and I kept that promise. I dreamt of being in the 'music business' and being able to go backstage and hang with these pop stars. I also went along to pop video shoots as a fan or extra. There was the ABC Movie called *Mantrap*, directed by Julian Templeton and the Wham! *Wake Me Up Before You Go Go* one at the Brixton Academy – directed by Andy Morahan, who I am proud to call my friend today. If you freeze-frame at the right moment you can see me amongst all the girls at the front.

It was in 1982 that a single came out called *Love Plus One* by a band called Haircut 100; I was aware of their first release *Favourite Shirts* which I liked a lot, but *Love Plus One* grabbed me. I don't know why… the guitar sound at the beginning, the melody, the singer was cool. He mumbled gibberish in interviews and I identified with his look; it was close to my aspirations. I quickly became a super fan. Their one and only album *Pelican West* can still cheer me up today 40 years later and they have just reunited. My brother Paul and I, along with a gaggle of girls, went to meet the band once or twice, and they signed all the stuff we put in front of them. Being a fan of the Haircuts was also a way of meeting girls – I felt like I was the only boy fan. I got friendly with and spoke on the phone a lot to Patsy Kensit. She starred in the *Nobody's Fool* video and Nick gave me the hat he wore in that film (I have lost it since, in one of many house moves). *I love(d) Haircut 100!* could well be the name of a documentary I plan to make around about the same time as writing this book.

I still wanted to be a DJ and by then had started my mobile disco called "Night Life" after the Thin Lizzy album. The logo was inspired heavily by the album's artwork. I was allowed to spend my Barmitzvah money on a mobile disco set-up and some lights, and my first gig was in Hatch End at Micky Finns wine bar. I got £25 a session. I had half an ice cream carton's worth of 7" singles and got away with it for months. All the money went on more records. I was soon doing kids' parties and getting well paid. I wasn't old enough to drive yet, so had to get a cabbie with an estate car to drive me to and from the gigs. The money went up and the gigs were happening regularly. I was on my way. My career had begun.

I possibly cheated my way through six O-Level passes by writing tiny notes on small pieces of paper. This was actually a revision technique, but I decided to hide the notes in my sweaty palm and cheat in at least history, if not more exams. I passed my O-Levels and wanted to just get on with my DJ career. I was earning great money, much more than my friends, and I didn't see the point in college or A-Levels. My parents convinced me to go to Cassio College in Watford to do a diploma in business. I couldn't argue with their "something to fall back on" logic and, after all, music was a business….

That summer before college started, I was immersing myself in golf, walking the one-mile journey to the club every day with Dad's old clubs on my back. I bought a Mars bar and blackcurrant and lemonade every day in the bar. I practised hard, had the occasional lesson with Mark and played 18 holes daily for about six weeks, getting my handicap down to about 17, where it has stayed practically ever since. I remember one day on the 17th hole, I was alone, and I took a whopping great swing with my two wood (at that age, all you want to do is whack the ball as far as it will go) and felt an enormous TWANG in my neck. At first, I thought I had been shot by an airgun. I fell to the floor screaming. There was no one about at all; I was scared. I rubbed my neck hard and slowly realised it must have been a muscle spasm and after about a minute lying in the grass, got up and walked home. Honestly, I've had trouble with my neck ever since and still regularly have osteo treatments and massages.

I failed my driving test a few times and also managed to crash Mum's Mini Metro whilst they were out. My brother Paul called me from up the road, literally at the top of our road, a two-minute drive and asked me to pick him up. So what does this teenage moron say to himself? I've not passed, it's not legal… sure, "I'll be there in a minute." Whizzing down the road in Mum's car, another car in front slows down almost to a stop. What the fuck are they doing? I think to myself. I'll just go around them – idiots. Of course, they were turning right into their driveway as any experienced driver would have known. BASH – 'FUCK!'.

I had to wait up for Mum and Dad to come home. I opened the door to them and was looking a nice shade of green-grey. "Something terrible has happened," I said… "What? What?" said Dad, clearly thinking someone had died, so when I told him I'd crashed the car, he was momentarily relieved. Said relief only lasted a minute or so and the result was I had to pay for my own driving lessons from there on in and he wasn't buying me a car. I took the punishment and thought I had gotten off lightly. What an idiot, what a typical teenager. When I started college I had to initially get the train there thanks to this setback.

Andrew Ridgeley of Wham! fame was in the year above me at Cassio and always played early Wham! records in the youth wing before they had their first hit. I was firm friends with two Janes at Cassio, they were both very pretty but we were just friends. I also became close with Danielle Finlay and Lisette Gatsky. I had first met Lisette when I was 13 in Stanmore where we both lived; her family then moved to Hatch End where I lived and our friendship grew. Really weirdly they then moved to Northwood as did we and then we went to the same college. Decisions made completely independently. Lisette and I are great friends today and she is my oldest friendship at over 45 years and we recently both sold our businesses at the same time. So weird how our lives have been so similar for so long (we both ended up in production as well)… Danielle tragically lost her mother when we were 17 and I had to go to my first ever funeral which was a grounding experience. I was there at her Jewish Shiva house (like a wake) every night and became good friends with her whole family, who were lovely. I was late one night as I HAD to go and see Culture Club at the Lyceum on The Strand – this band blew my mind, they were unique and had just got to No.1 in the charts with their debut single *Do You Really Wanna Hurt Me*. Boy George was fantastic, I thought their songs were brilliant and George's voice was on a different level to everyone else around at that time. I ended up seeing Culture Club more than any other band at the time – I loved them.

Danielle was a Barry Manilow nut. She took me to my first Manilow show at Blenheim Palace (the One Voice tour) which blew me away; what a voice he had. I wasn't afraid to love any music that stirred me… later in my life, I got to know Boy George well as my brother ended up managing him and Culture Club, and I would also later have a bizarre encounter with Barry Manilow when I started to film shows in the early nineties.

I passed my driving test and promptly bought my first car with my own money. It was a green Ford Escort estate, it had a huge boot that fitted all my disco gear in and the seats folded down, which made a brilliant, if not a slightly uncomfortable, place to get to know girls more intimately.

Chapter 4

Last Night a DJ Saved My Life

Indeep

I got Saturday jobs in a butchers, picking up the waste, chicken windpipes and giblets from sawdust and making freezing cold mincemeat out of, well, anything really. I worked in a garage behind my Mum's clothes shop which was called Spangles in Hatch End, where I learnt how to clean spanners and why yucky Swarfega was used to clean my hands. Also in a hardware store – I love a good hardware store today. I also worked at Dad's video rental shop called Cosmic Culture in Harrow on the Hill and, relatively speaking, I always seemed to have money in my pocket.

But most importantly, I DJ'ed whenever I was hired. I was determined that my future lay behind the twin decks playing music that I loved and entertaining people. I practised my autograph all over books, desecrating them and I kept building my record collection and pop music knowledge by reading the music papers and listening to Radio 1. I knew every record in the charts and every Tuesday, I would listen at lunchtime to those charts on Radio 1 in my car in the carpark at Cassio College. I always tuned into Gary Crowley's Tuesday Club on Capital Radio; it was essential listening.

My record collection was growing and my feeling as to what people wanted to hear or dance to was instinctive. I also had a good microphone technique. I was a bloody good DJ. I got myself sorted with basic contracts for gigs, got deposits from clients, which helped with cash flow and developed a small fanbase of young school girls. I got a professional photo card made and printed and gave them away at gigs. At last I was signing autographs! I created commercial gigs in Edgware and Stanmore, using my name in the ads; I charged £3 to get in and made a few hundred quid each time. I made enough money to be able to go into town and buy the clothes my favourite pop stars were wearing, expensive clothes. You know the saying "clothes maketh the man", well that's how I felt. I spent £500 on a John Richmond jacket that

I LOVED, shirts that Nick Heyward wore, or jeans from Woodhouse that George and Andrew from Wham! wore, sweat bottoms from BOY on the Kings Road etc. Life was great; I was even enjoying college.

I met my friend, Julian Spalter, at Cassio. He says I just walked up to him and asked him if he wanted to go away that summer to Majorca… I don't remember, but it's possible. Girls were everywhere and having come from an all-boys school to a college with a hairdressing and beauty wing, it was like walking into Aphrodite's Den…. There was one girl I had the hots for, but she wouldn't look at me at the college disco when I asked her to dance, she simply said "No", not even "No thanks" or "Not right now", just "No!" – I was crushed. I lifted myself out of this moment of love and decided that my heart was too precious to get broken, so I proceeded into what became years of one-night stands. Not that I had had actual sex yet. I was a late starter when it came to that.

Prior to that planned summer holiday, which was almost a year away, I went to Marbella with Mum and Dad and my brothers and, as I was old enough, I was allowed to hang in Puerto Banus with friends I had down there. My parents had a small private timeshare flat, so we went to that part of the world quite regularly. I used to make mix tapes for some of the bars in return for free drinks and one night in Captain Baylors, a bar in Puerto Banus, there was a woman, not a girl, a woman. Oh my god, she was so sexy and must have been at least five years older than me. I was a skinny thing, but I had cool clothes, the gift of the gab and free drinks. One thing led to another and at about 2am it was clear that tonight was the night.

I was petrified that it would all be over too quickly, so just before I went to her flat, I went back to mine and took care of the inevitable in about seven seconds. I was so excited. When it came to the first time, I lasted ages – what a great instinctive strategy that was… in fact, I lasted so long that she kept asking what she could do for me. I had absolutely no idea what to say, she had probably just had enough. Here I was in a dream scenario aged 17 and I didn't know what to say to this very sexy lady… when I told her in the early hours that was my first time, she was flabbergasted. I don't really talk about sex ever, it's a private matter, but I'm sure my first time was a far superior event compared to two sixteen-year-olds 'working it out'. I was hooked; older women were the way forward on so many levels.

That summer, Julian, myself and a very strange boy

called Simon went to Magaluf; it was like an episode of *The Inbetweeners*, clubs, drinks, friends and older women… there was one older Jewish lady from Leeds, oh no… I don't *really* talk about sex, sorry… but it was a seriously great holiday.

Later that year, I graduated with distinction from a course that included accounting and typewriting – an HND in business studies. It was mildly gratifying and settled Mum and Dad down, but that was it, I was going to go full-time into professional DJ'ing.

The local gigs continued, but I was getting bored of them, so instead of not doing them at all, I simply doubled my price, did half as many, and still earned the same dough. I upgraded my car to a Suzuki Jeep with a great tape player and Julian and I were firm, if not best mates. He introduced me to the world of Edgware becks (I'm not really sure how to explain what a beck is, so ask a Jewish friend please). The scene was nonsense but I made friends during this period who are still my friends today over 40 years later.

In business, as in life, you have to have a radar and listen to what your gut tells you. One time back then, I was doing a gig in a smart restaurant in Highgate. It was someone's son's Barmitzvah, and a sixth sense told me I was going to have trouble getting paid. I got the sense that this man was swimming way out of his depth with this party. Nevertheless, I did the job and sure enough he 'forgot his chequebook'. "Call me in the week," he said. I did, and he never picked up. I called the restaurant to see if they had any problems getting paid and they were also being 'knocked'. I'll never forget driving home from golf one Sunday and calling my Dad to tell him that, for the first time ever, a client was trying to knock me for the money. "Son," said Dad, "you are going to have to put this one down to experience." I was raging… fuck that, I thought and drove straight round in my muddy golf clothes to the client's family home. The wife answered the door and explained that her husband was out. "No problem," I said, "I'll wait" and I sat outside their home in my car for over an hour. He came back and I confronted him about getting paid; he said he didn't have any cash on him and let me in – he was being very slippery yet nice. "Would you like some tea?" he said. "No thanks, just the money you owe me." "I need to go to the cash machine, I'll get it to you later in the week," he smiled. "I'm not going anywhere without my money," I retorted and sat at their kitchen table, as his wife smiled nervously. He went out to get the cash, came back and gave me £250 of the £300 he owed me.

"That's all I could get," he said. "I'm not moving until I get it all," I said defiantly. His wife glared at him and then another fifty magically appeared from his pocket. There are knockers in this world and you have to stand up to them; they are bullies and they have no scruples. If you want to get paid for work you have done and they delay and delay, you have to go in hard and that applies in much bigger businesses too. Trust your gut and act on it. I called Dad after and said, "Fuck putting it down to experience, Dad; I got my money," and told him what had happened. A mild-mannered accountant, I was not!

Aged 17, I had a Saturday job with Julian and his brother Daryl at a fashion outlet called Chevy in Golders Green. We got a great discount on the clothes which were very fashionable amongst us lot back then. The High Street in Golders Green was a hubbub of activity for kids my age and we had a lot of fun.

My first full-time professional nightclub DJ gig was at a brand new club called Shaftesbury's on the Avenue, just under the Trocadero in London. I blagged it. By now, I had a huge record collection, but I really wasn't experienced enough to be in a top West End nightclub. I told them I could run my own Thursday night and that I had a following which would bring in the punters; they believed me. I shat myself at the prospect of pulling this off but put a nice big press ad in the Jewish Chronicle, and it worked. The huge hair and espadrilles crowd from my manor flocked to the West End. We had a hit on our hands, and I was a real, professional nightclub disc jockey.

I went on to play in lots of clubs in the West End back then, places like The Park in Kensington, Samantha's (where I met and hung with Jeffrey Daniel from Shalamar. Jeffrey was the man who taught Micheal Jackson to moonwalk!). I got the jobs at these clubs by promoting the nights myself and getting the becky kids to go down; it all worked and much fun was had, particularly for my friend, Julian Spalter, who enjoyed standing by me in the DJ box until he spotted a girl he fancied. He would go down for a ridiculous over-exaggerated dance, only to return an hour later having routinely not pulled. I also DJ'ed at Middlesex and Herts (we called it Sex and Tarts.) This was our local club and I did Thursday nights along with other kids I knew who were on the Banana Split mobile disco roster that Julian Posner ran. Dean, Paul and Stephen still DJ today, I believe.

I was still doing the private gigs and one such gig was for a 12-year-old girl in Moor Park. Her family home was huge and I did what I did in those days and the kids had a blast. When it came to getting paid, her father proffered a giant-sized cheque with the logo of Utopia Studios emblazed across it. I promptly said, "I don't want the money, just a summer job at your recording studio." The dad was Phil Wainman, he laughed and said take the money, you can have a summer job as well, but he thought my DJ'ing was really good, a little special he said and he wanted to manage me. Fuck. Brilliant. I had no real idea who Phil was at this point or indeed what Utopia was.

I went down to see Phil a few weeks later towards the end of my time at college – Utopia was the real deal. There were pictures of Stevie Wonder, Mick Jagger, Sting and all sorts adorning the reception area. Phil introduced me to a man called Newton Wills who said he wanted to manage me. Newton was nice and also looked after a singer called Sam Brown and MTV star Downtown Julie Brown. He introduced me to one of my heroes, Peter Powell the Radio 1 DJ – we went to Pete's house by the River Thames and I saw all his gold and platinum discs from the likes of Duran Duran, Human League, Depeche Mode, and so many more. We chatted in his back garden and he gave me his wise words of experience and wisdom. I did have my suspicions about Peter and Newton but nothing untoward ever happened so it was probably just my overactive imagination.

Utopia was the best job I could have imagined at the age of 17. I played drums in a pop video for the blonde singer from Tight Fit called Julie Harris (swoon), I tape op'ed for a band called Reflex as they recorded their hit *The Politics of Dancing*. I remember walking in on Kajagoogoo's front man Limhal holding hands with Radio 1's Paul Gambaccini in the remix room (nothing nowadays, but something much more back then), I never said a word to anyone (ever) until now. The remix room was run, when I was there, by a producer called Tim Palmer; he was so rock-a-billy cool and quite brilliant as his career many years later proved; he was also super nice to me.

Probably the highlight of my few weeks there was when the band Madness came in to record the B-side to their hit, *Wings of a Dove*. The writing and recording was an organic process; I'm sure they didn't have any preconceived notion of what the tune would be, and so the band would just jam and build the tracks. They decided to call it *Behind the 8 Ball*. There was a pool table a few yards from Studio 2 and I was despatched to set up a mic on a boom stand and bring the lead back to the desk. The engineer was called Mark; he was impossibly cool and handsome with long blonde hair. He looked more like a pop star than an engineer. He and the band agreed to let me break the balls to create the sound that would end up on the record, which I duly did. I had to hide my excitement with feigned professionalism. That track still exists and is a testament to my time at Utopia Studios. I am still in touch with Phil, who I later discovered was a legendary producer in his own right. He created the famous twin drum set sound and produced bands like The Sweet and The Bay City Rollers. He also produced one of my all-time favourite records *I Don't Like Mondays* by The Boomtown Rats, which stayed at No.1 for weeks. A true mentor.

Chapter 5

London Calling

The Clash

At the end of my time at Cassio, Mr Seabrook, our lovely accounts lecturer, got me some work experience at Music Sales. He was so kind and nice to all of us. I loved Music Sales; the office was on Frith Street in Soho and I was a runner. I worked in the post room with Mick, a spotty, ginger rocker and just did as I was told.

Going out to get Mr Wise, the owner of Music Sales, a coffee, walking past hookers all the time who asked me if I wanted any business, I couldn't work it out at first, then Mick explained. Ergggh, I wondered why anyone would pay for sex with someone on the street. Bob Wise was a nice man and always looked up and gave me a warm smile when I bought in his coffee. I didn't realise it at the time but he was a legend as well, a multi-millionaire music publisher who found a niche in the music business selling sheet music; so clever. I loved that job and stayed there for a couple of months.

I decided that, whilst building my DJ career, I wanted to work for a record company. Yeah, that would work, so I wrote to every single one, eighty three of them. My CV was good for my age; I had the passion, the smarts and some good experience. I was also willing to start from the very bottom. I got rejected by every single one of them and I still have all the letters to prove it. Who cares? Fuck 'em, I thought; I could still earn a living in music and DJ'ing was where it was at for me, more money, more fun and like the song goes, *easy girls and late nights, cigarettes and love bites.*

I'm not sure my parents were enthusiastic at all but they gave me the space to give it a go. Everything was going ok, but I still had plenty of time on my hands, particularly during the day. Passing my driving test opened up the universe, well, London, which as far as I was concerned, was the universe. As a family, we had moved even further out to a place called Northwood; it was 21 miles from Central London but it was a great flat and my parents had special record drawers made for my collection.

I took a part-time job at Benetton in Brent Cross. Benetton was a famous Europe-wide jumper shop and I was a sales assistant. We learnt to fold a jumper within a millimetre of its life and then sold them. One day, this hot older lady came in, and as quick as a flash, I was by her side, "Can I help you?" "Just looking," came the reply. I recognised her; she lived in The Avenue, a road I walked down every day in Hatch End for years, to get the bus or train to school or work.

At this point, I have to admit to something so ridiculous that it embarrasses me still to this day. When I was 14 or 15 and working at Wembley Market, I'd walk down that road at about 5 am, this lady had a house with a huge Pampas grass bush in the middle of the front garden; it featured these incredible flowers that looked like giant feather dusters – it was magnificent. So what did I do? As an act of utterly ridiculous vandalism, every week, I would take one of those feather dusters out! I'd cut it off and then chuck it over the railway bridge. It was 5 am, dark and no one would see. It was moronic, I did it every week until there were none left. What was I thinking? I felt terrible at the sight of all the feather dusters gone, even remorseful and here was the sexy lady who lived there.

She wanted to try on a jumper or two, so I showed her to the dressing room at the back. She went in and I stayed just outside in case she wanted a different size or colour. I swear she left a gap in the curtain on purpose. I tried not to look but to me she was a woman of fantasy and I was sure she was flirting and did it on purpose. I saw her bra and boobs, blimey… exciting. Then she took her bra off; I looked away (IDIOT! Why?) then she came out wearing this jumper with a huge slit at the back, the wrong way round – her magnificent cleavage on full show. I told her it was the wrong way round."Oh, silly me," she giggled and bought it anyway. I couldn't find the space, courage or moment to say, "Don't you live in Hatch End? Fancy a drink one night?" I think she must have been in her thirties and was so sexy. As I type this, I realise she's probably in her late 70s; I hope she lived a great life.

Whilst at Benetton I heard about a job for a DJ on Saturdays for Radio Top Shop in the same shopping centre as Benetton, Brent Cross. This was a dream job; I could refine my radio DJ skills and get ready for superstardom. All I needed was my records, my natural talent and I'd smash it. I got the job. The decks were in a broom cupboard in the basement, the room was tiny and I had to be in there playing tunes and making up shit to say for eight hours every Saturday. What a job! The novelty wore off fairly quickly, but they loved me. I made the staff laugh and they loved the music, so they asked me to do early evenings as well. I lasted about six months but couldn't take it anymore; it was so claustrophobic and I was better than that. I had other gigs where I earned a lot more money, so fuck it, I left.

Newton, my manager, got me a gig DJ'ing at The Grand Palace Hotel in Stockholm, Sweden; it was to be a very early form of 'satellite' link up with the Camden Palace in London. I loved that place and often went to spot the pop stars on a Tuesday night. It wasn't really a satellite link up, more a phone line plugged into the back of the desk.

When I arrived in Stockholm, I was picked up at the airport and felt like a pop star. They got me a room at the five-star Grand Palace Hotel and took me out the night before the gig to the most bizarre club. I was ushered in through the kitchen, as prior to 11pm, it was ladies only, and they were watching a *Magic*

Mike-type strip show and drinking freely. The idea was that by 11pm they would be tipsy and perhaps a little horny for when the club let the boys in. I got in early and had a great night; imagine having a room at the five-star hotel around the corner! The gig went off great and I had such a good time, then it was back to earth and London.

Soon after leaving radio Top Shop, I saw a job advertised for an assistant VJ at a place called the Video Cafe. I went up to the West End for the interview with the head VJ; I wasn't even sure what a VJ was, it was just before MTV got massive, but it was essentially DJ'ing with videos. The place was amazing but the bloke who interviewed me and would potentially be my boss was an idiot. How was he more qualified to do this than me? I got the job and was thrilled.

I used to drive up every day and in those days could park right outside in Argyle Street, (the Cafe was underneath the London Palladium) for just a few pennies in the meter. The general manager was a man called Gary Davies (not the DJ, who I would soon be friendly with). Gary and I got along and because this bloke Neil, the head VJ, was a lazy, fat twat (you could say that back then), I got to programme the music and present/VJ all the time. Within a matter of weeks, Gary fired Neil and promoted me and I got to hire my own assistant. I chose one of my good friends, Michael Jacobs. Michael was a couple of years younger than me and in those days he didn't quite have the work ethic required. He was supposed to set shit up for me by getting in early and doing what was required. I'd often catch him just sitting there reading The Sun having done fuck all in his first few hours of work. By the way, today Mike is a super successful businessman, still one of my best friends and still annoying! Anyway one of his jobs was to prepare clips for our pop video quiz and load the questions into the Aston character generator, which is effectively a video typewriter. We created a nightly in-house pop TV show and I'd be out there with the mic being the 'personality'. So there I was in the middle of this huge venue, the Video Cafe. It was a massive success and we'd have queues around the block most weekends. This particular night, it was full in the main room, about 200 people. I read out the questions that had been prepared and later, when it was time for the answers, we used video captions and photos or video clips to give the answers. I read out one question from the screen in front of the packed house that Michael had typed up earlier… "Who turned black at the age of five?" Gasps went up. I turned on my heels to stare at Mike and he just ducked down behind the console. Moron. I explained to the audience that I thought that was meant to read, "Who turned blind at the aged of five?" As I said that, Mike flicked up a picture of Ray Charles.

The Video Cafe was amazing… it shot to huge status in London and was the 'in' place for the kids to hang. The food was crap, chicken burgers so dry you could break your teeth on them, but it was BUZZING most nights of the week. So many famous people came down to eat and watch the show. I was a big Wham! fan by now and played their videos all the time and George Michael came to a party at the Cafe for the first time sporting a beard! It made the front pages of the national tabloid press. A-ha came down. All the kids from my way and my friends followed me there. I met and befriended Curiosity Killed The Cat at a Super Bowl party. I had two assistants in the end, Anthony, who met and dated Letitia Dean from *Eastenders* and Roman, who was the best joint roller in London, and we often slid off to the maintenance room for a cheeky smoke. We had guest DJs from Capital Radio and even Shirley and Pepsi from Wham! had a slot every Thursday night. I had exclusive video content that I beg stole and borrowed including a really early copy of *Motown at The Apollo*.

What a show that was! George Michael sang with Stevie Wonder and Smokey Robinson, Boy George with Luther Vandross, Rod Stewart tore the house down with Otis Redding's *Sitting on the Dock of the Bay*. The Commodores version of *Nightshift* still gives me shivers and the battle of the bands starring The Four Tops and The Temptations is still today one of the best musical performances ever – look it up on YouTube. No one had this material, there was no YouTube back then, so people came to expect the best music on our screens, video footage you couldn't see or hear elsewhere in the UK, and it worked. We were phenomenally busy and those that were there will always remember it.

The head of the security firm that looked after the Video Cafe was a man called Alfie Weaver. Alf was a legend and in those days M&A were the main firm in London for security. Since the sixties, he'd always looked after Frank Sinatra when he came to the UK and Frank was on his way to London to do a small tour with Sammy Davies Jnr and Liza Minelli. Mike and I really wanted to see the show but the tickets were so expensive and of course it was sold out. "Don't worry boys," said Alfie, "just come to the stage door and wear dickie bows." Ok, we did just that; when we arrived we knew all the security guys from the Video Cafe and Alfie gave us two security passes. It was 1989 and a security pass looked like one of those passes you get when you visit a low rent office. "Pop that on and go wherever you want."… we took the piss. We went backstage, walking with confidence as if it were an everyday occurrence. Come showtime, Mike and I stood either side of the Royal Albert Hall stage with our backs touching the stage. There was no one in the entire place that was closer to the action than us. At one point, Frank stood about two feet from me. I even took my fake role seriously and gestured to an over-enthusiastic fan who wanted to get up to stay seated. We were kids but somehow got away with it. I remember afterwards not quite believing what had happened; I had just seen Frank Sinatra sing in person. Thanks Alf… he's long gone now but he wrote a "kiss and tell" book about Frank that I must dig out.

Without doubt, the most embarrassing moment of my life happened late one night at the Video Cafe. The night was done, it was a Saturday and the place had been mobbed. I was sat in reception chatting to Gary, the general manager. He asked me how the night went and I said it was great except for this really annoying Scottish hostess who kept standing on my console stage. "Which one?" he asked with a grin. "It's not funny," I snapped, "You know what one, the fucking Scottish one with the big hair and big arse." He started laughing. I told him again that it wasn't funny and he said, "I'm not sure which one you mean?" I then launched into a tirade of abuse about this hostess. Gary was on the floor laughing at my passionate regaling of this girl and then remarked, "What, her?" I turned around and leaning over listening to every word I'd said was this annoying hostess. I turned back to Gary and quickly snapped, "No, not her." "But we've only got one Scottish hostess!" he replied. If the earth could have swallowed me up....

This should have been a life lesson right there and then. It became one a few years later when I was talking on a mobile phone about leaving my job and starting up on my own. A lovely client of mine called when I got off the train and said, "So you're leaving?" I hadn't told a soul of my plans, except for the person I was talking to on the phone. It turned out Nigel, my client, was sitting in the bay behind me on the train and had heard every word. Ever since that day, whether I'm in a restaurant, on a plane or train, I always look fully around me to see who might be listening. My brain and mouth seem to work in tandem; in other words I tend to speak without thinking first.

Chapter 6

America

Neil Diamond

One day at The Video Cafe, after Michael had already left to build his fortune in the greeting cards business, I was preparing by myself. It was extremely quiet at 4 pm and there was tall, stocky man just looking around quite intently – he was by the VJ studio and I asked him if he needed any help. This was a pivotal moment in my life; I might have ignored him and then what was to transpire might never had happened.

His name was Craig Saunders and he was a heart surgeon from Bakersfield in California about 100 miles north of Los Angeles. He thought the concept of the Video Cafe was amazing and he already had plans to open a sports-themed restaurant in

Bakersfield with further plans to then open up more across the west coast of America. He asked if I would be interested in helping. Would I? Errr yes… "What do you know about this man?" my parents enquired later. Only what he'd told me and that he would pay for my flights and I could give it a go.

Within a couple of weeks, I took a leave of absence from London and flew for the first time to LA. Madness in hindsight but it all turned out to be true. I would stay at Craig's enormous house; his wife and family had all moved out, his kids had grown up and flown the nest and he was divorced. He had a pool room and I had a wing of this mansion to myself. His business partner permanently lent me his Thunderbird car and I was up and down to LA helping to set up and buy the equipment with an engineer friend called Ian Sweet; they could never pronounce Ian in California, they kept calling him "eye-an". What a blast! George Michael was No.1. with *Faith* and I was listening to Kiss100 up and down the I-5 freeway. I remember one day early on having a meeting with Craig and his partner, David, in a Mr Whippy downtown. As we sat in the booth by the window, we heard a crack on the window. Someone had driven by and fired an airgun through the window and the pellet whizzed past our three faces. WTAF?

I was freaked out, but stayed on despite this frightening moment.

Craig always called the motorbike riders out there 'donors'; he was a heart surgeon and one day asked me if I'd like to see him work first-hand. Sure, why not? I thought. You cannot prepare yourself for being two feet away from a patient who has his chest sawn open with a medical angle grinder, his ribcage clamped open, then watching your friend take out veins from the patient's legs and meticulously replace arteries in the patient's heart. It was mind-blowing. The smell of the burning bones as he sawed will never leave me. About two weeks later, this old boy – the patient – came to see Craig at the restaurant with only the aid of a walking stick. Wow.

Shagnasty's (I kid you not), the video and sport restaurant, was a huge success; people queued for ages to get in and after dinner and the playing of some pop videos from me, it became a club with yours truly 'spinning the wheels of steel'.

There are a few fun stories about my time in California in 1987. I loved the girls and there were a few lovely waitresses that I became better acquainted with, one even took me home, failing to mention she had recently broken up with one of the managers from Shagnasty's. I was asleep when he burst into her bedroom and had a complete meltdown. Thankfully, I remembered he knew me and we got along, which probably saved me from a pounding.

I still had a penchant for the older lady and one night ended up with a very sexy hairdresser. I had been in the States for several weeks and hadn't had a haircut yet, so she offered a nice place to sleep for the night and a cut; how could I refuse? As I sat down for the haircut, I was nervous; I think her salon was more for the blue rinse brigade and not a trendy London DJ. She proceeded to butcher my hair and I quickly said, "Just a little trim please," and managed to avert complete disaster. After I asked politely how much did I owe, she replied, "No, don't be silly." I politely insisted a second time hoping she would say "no" again, but she responded, "Ok, $25." 25 fucking bucks for a shit haircut in those days was a lot of money. Object lesson learnt – if anyone offered me anything free in the future I would say, "Thank you very much" and smile. I stayed in California for about six months and had a great time. I had a small love affair with a Greek nurse called Stephanie who ended up coming to London later that year; an invite I regretted very soon after she arrived. Another very short-lived affair.

Back in London, I was about 22 years old and apart from the girl at college who rebuffed me, I never had strong feelings for anyone in particular and didn't really date; I couldn't as my work hours were so unsociable. Then along came Jane. She was out for the night with some friends; one thing led to another. She took me back to her place and therein lies the main thrust of this story. As we approached this dark driveway in Kensington, she leaned over and said "It's alright, George, it's me", "Oh, hi Jane," came the response from a policeman in the shadows of a small hut. There was no barrier as such. We drove down this long gravel driveway; I had absolutely no idea where I was. I turned left into a small mews and we had a wonderful night. I liked Jane and it turned out that I was in the staff quarters of Kensington Palace. When I left the next morning, I was very surprised where I was. Jane told me she was on the staff of the Prince and Princess of Wales. WHAT?

So began a passionate if not short-lived affair. We stayed together with secret dates for a couple of months, during which time I was poached from the Video Cafe and ask to be the main DJ at Le Palais Hammersmith, which was to have a huge celebrity opening party with the Prince and Princess attending after a Princes Trust gig at Wembley. It was a star-studded affair. I asked Jane what kind of music the Prince liked and she asked his butler who said that earlier that week he had been dispatched to Our Price records in Kensington High Street to buy a Pointer Sisters record. When I left Jane's mews staff flat that morning, I saw, for the first and only time, Diana, the Princess of Wales on the doorstep of the Palace; cue an extended stare from me and a stare back from her. She was dressed in one of those velour tracksuits in a bronze colour; I was gobsmacked.

Later that night, the royal couple arrived at the Palais. I had premiered the new George Michael video for *I Want Your Sex* and there were tabloid stories about the royal couple in sexy George video scandal which was bollocks as I didn't play it when they were there. Anyway they arrived, greeted a line-up of pop stars and then came down the stairs right by my DJ box. I swear Diana stared at me and in my head she said, "Where have I seen you before?" Obviously I stared back, it was only a second or three, but quite the thrill.

I had put on a 12" Pointer Sisters track when they arrived and the Prince said during his speech that he wished this particular venture at The Palais great success and if we kept playing music like tonight, in particular The Pointer Sisters, they would be back tomorrow night. It was a great story and I have the video of the walk, the stare and the speech – I'll show you if you pop over.

I then got a call from my old boss at the Video Cafe – Gary Davies – and he asked me if I wanted to go over to Sweden (again) and open a franchised Video Cafe in Linköping, not too far from Stockholm; not too far in miles maybe but it was a sleepy town, a few thousand miles from Stockholm culturally. I said yes, I'd love to. I enjoyed setting up the Video Cafe and stayed on for about three months to VJ/DJ. I also got myself a slot on the local radio station (they approached me at the Video Cafe) and did a show I called *The Hurdy Gurdy Show* (a little disrespectful, but I don't think they had *The Muppets* in Sweden at that time). I became a minor celebrity in Linköping and the surrounding towns, attracting fan mail and queues at the Video Cafe. I made some great friends there, two girls (just friends), Karen and Karen, who let me hang with them and their friends. I went skiing for the first time since that horrible accident, had countless liaisons with lovely ladies and attracted my first and only ever super-fan. She followed me around a bit which I didn't really mind, she was super pretty but way too young for me!

After about three months, I returned to London and I managed to find a way to carry on the radio show by sending out quarter-inch tapes every week. I recorded the shows at BFBS Radio in Paddington. BFBS was and still is the worldwide radio service for the British Forces and all the top DJs had shows. I got myself a tape op job there and they let me record my show in a spare studio. I met all the top DJs – Nicky Horne, Richard Allison, and Gary Crowley. Later in life, I would work with all these boys as my career progressed, but back then, I seemed to hit it off with Crowley the best. We were similar ages and he was THE hip pop radio and club DJ with his nightly shows on Capital Radio.

Gary Davies let me come back to the Video Cafe after my travels, but it was never the same as the first couple of years. I hadn't given up on my hope of being a famous DJ and I managed to get a screen test for new satellite TV station called Music Box. I got down to the last two after a ridiculously long day and lost out to a soon-to-be minor celebrity presenter called Gaz Top. The shame of it was, the exec producer who became a great friend and mentor said I had a sharp "s" in my sibilance when I spoke, like a whistle. I did have a small gap between my front teeth, but really? Fucking Gaz, who I also stayed mates with for quite a while had a bloody full-on lisp! I let it go.

I was still gigging, doing the private parties, at least I thought I was. When I came home from America, I went up to my room and all my disco gear had disappeared. "Mum! Where are my decks and my speakers?" She had no idea; it seems that whilst I was away, my middle brother Paul, who was about 18, began his lifelong love of gambling (he might have stopped now actually), in fact, his style and penchant for risk saw him build up a property portfolio of over £500m in the early 00s and he became Vice Chairman at Spurs. Anyway, it seemed he'd gone to a casino in Luton with his idiot friend Spencer, lost all his money and he thought it would be a good idea to pawn my disco gear, win the money back and get my decks back before I got home. Even now whilst typing this I can't believe he did it and got away with it… another one who has been getting away with it all his life… I can only imagine when I got back I thought I was too far into the professional nightclub/video cafe gigs and that these decks were a thing of the past.

By this time, I'd been asked by this chap whose name I just can't remember to DJ for his roadshow called Omega Powerhouse. Why not? It was good dough and the equipment he had was incredible with a big lighting rig, massive sound system and a big old 3 tonne truck. I just said ok and before I knew it we had gigs up and down the country. When I think about it now, I had never played outside of London (apart from America and Sweden) and the provinces were a new experience. I was going to places like Hull, Grimsby, Swindon and doing gigs where they had put me on posters outside town halls as a star-named DJ from London. It was fake news, I never saw myself as well-known. I used to get into the truck with these smelly roadie types, in my flash London clothes, travel to Alschwartzyarn (more Yiddish, meaning 'the middle of fucking nowhere'). They'd set up and I'd go out the front where there were posters with my name on them and queues of girls waiting to get in. It was a bloody con, I wasn't famous, but fuck it, I played the role, handed out photos, signed them and then got back in the smelly truck to drive back to Northolt where their lock-up was. It was a mad period and in the end I hated the travelling and the money seemed not fair as I was pulling the crowds in, so I gave it up.

I started to hang a bit with Gary Crowley, going to Capital Radio on the Euston Road, where his producer let me make my radio DJ reel in the studio next to GC using Capital jingles. I later discovered his producer might have had ulterior motives; my gaydar in those days wasn't as on point as it is today. Gary and I and his friends, Andros (George Michael's cousin) and close friend, Simon Halfon (George's good friend and record sleeve designer) used to go to his club in Rayners Lane (just up the road from my old school and where that infamous drug bust happened!). I felt part of the 'it' crowd. I'm happy to say that both GC and Simon are still my friends today; I even ended up hiring Simon's son Joe (who I love) recently as an editor.

I was still on my second stint at the Video Cafe and often went out after to the clubs with my friends. One night, I was invited along with Simon to Stringfellows with George Michael. I'd never met George properly and at this time he was quickly becoming one of the biggest stars in the world. It was a great night. Shirley and Pepsi were my friends from working together at The Cafe and they were there too. My god, this was social climbing and I wasn't even trying. I ended up on the dance floor with George, Shirley and others near to closing time; I had to metaphorically pinch myself. We all left together and I tagged along until Emanuel's, a late-night restaurant on the Finchley Road, was deemed to be potentially 'full of piss-heads' by George and we all went our separate ways;

I went in anyway and grabbed a burger, I was starving.

George and I went on to a couple more encounters over the years but they'll come much later. This group of trendy friends endured. I remember a house party at Pepsi and her boyfriend Matt's flat and they were all there, but I never felt fully part of the group so slid back to my true friends, who were all by now congregating on Tuesday and Thursday nights at The Hippodrome in Leicester Square. I could join them after work at the Video Cafe at about 11pm.

The Hippodrome was the biggest and hippest nightclub in Europe at that time and I got friendly with one of the DJs there, Paul Myers. He and I became fast friends and one day, he recommended to his boss that I could be the VJ/DJ they were looking for. I had an interview and somehow got the gig. I think I had a bit of imposter syndrome at The Hippodrome. I was one of three main DJs, although I was the main VJ. Paul and Tony were proper DJs, their mixing skills were sublime, mine were more akin to Dewhurst (the master butcher) as Tony, a slightly mean queen, once dubbed me. Still, I knew my tunes and did my bit for just over a year until I was made redundant. My time at The Hippodrome was truly special; it was the late

80s, it's where I thought to myself… I had free drinks, I was surrounded by sexy nighttime people, I played records until 3am and got well paid. I also saw my friends all the time as they all came down. There is one great story from that time that I have to tell you about.

Whitney Houston, one of the biggest stars in the world, was on tour in the UK. One night, she came to the club with her huge entourage; she was in the VIP section right by our DJ stage and went down to the dance floor for a boogie. I wasn't playing so I stood by the ginormous lighting desk next to Marco, the young lighting jock and the junior member of the team. I think Paul was playing and, once he had mixed the next record, all four of us stood in a line vaguely trying to look busy by operating light switches but actually staring at Whitney. She kept glancing up at us. Out of the corner of our mouths we all said, "She's looking at me." "No she's not, she's looking at me," and then she beckoned me down to dance with her. "She's not asking you," Paul insisted, "she's asking me." So I mouthed, "Who me?" She wagged her finger, no, and pointed to Marco.

Now, Marco was beautiful; he was about 19 years old, with olive skin, fantastic black, curly hair; just a lovely, handsome guy. On a normal day, he was shy, but this sent him over the edge. "No fucking way, I'm not going down there." "You have to," we exclaimed, and in the end we had to physically push him off the stage and down he went. He was so awkward and couldn't bloody dance, so what did we do in the middle of the night in one of the biggest clubs in the world? We dropped the video screen, darkened the club, and played Whitney's *Where Do Broken Hearts Go*. We could have gotten into big trouble but it worked. Marco and Whitney danced like two fourteen year olds at a school disco. We had to go back to Cameo's *Word Up* straight after.

Marco ended up in the VIP section chatting to Whitney and then said he had to go back to work. When he came back on stage and we asked him, "Well?" he told us what he had said to her about having to get back to work. We sent him forcibly back to Whitney. It was a Saturday night and, via Marco, she invited us all down to Wembley Arena the next night to see her show. We had the best seats and she told thousands of fans that she had been to The Hippodrome last night, glancing up at us (well, Marco) and that she had such a good time. Marco went backstage afterwards and spent ages with her, while we waited patiently, but he was so shy and nothing happened.

One other small Marco story… we once recorded a TV show at The Hippodrome; it was called *Cliff at The Hip* (so naff) and the story was about one of Cliff Richard's special guests, the very successful band Five Star. All Marco had to do was press start on the smoke machine and stop when the director said so. Trouble was he took his headphones off after pressing start and didn't hear the director screaming "STOP!" The result is comedy genius and you can still see it on YouTube. To say he smoked them out would be an understatement. It was so funny; Paul and I were up in the gods operating the followspots in hysterics. I heard many years later from Paul that Marco died in a helicopter crash; this really shocked me, so these stories are for you, our friend. Such a lovely boy.

During my time at The Hippodrome, I met my one and only what I would call girlfriend; her name was also Jane and she was a transatlantic stewardess for BA. At first, she was just a 'pull' at The Hippodrome and back at hers in Windsor was lovely. So what started, and normally would have ended soon after, just carried on. Upon reflection, we had space, as she was always away and coming back together became more special. Our thing lasted over a year and we really liked each other. I don't even remember why it ended.

I think it was her as I was still keen, maybe I was too young. Many years later, whilst married, I bumped into Jane; it was a real shock for both of us. We had a big hug and went our separate ways. So if you ever read this, Jane, you really were my one and only real girlfriend (until I met my wife) and it was great.

As I mentioned, about one and a half years after starting at The Hippodrome, I was made redundant. "Last in, first out," the boss stated. Fuck! This was the first time in my life my work-life hadn't overlapped with the next exciting opportunity and I didn't have a job. Our boss was a guy called Phil Pyke; he was a good guy, not blessed with a great personality and I was pissed off when he made me redundant, but Phil taught me one of the greatest life lessons I ever learnt. As a critique at my exit interview, he said kindly that he thought I lacked a sense of urgency. I am sure he was right but in that moment I thought to myself, I'm a bloody DJ, what do you want from me? I never forgot his words and, from then on, a sense of urgency has been a massive part of who I am in my career and has definitely helped me in my endeavours throughout my life. Cheers Phil.

I was still living at home with Mum and Dad and my brothers in Northwood. I had spent years having breakfast in West End cafes at 4am, waking up at lunchtime, playing records, having fun and getting well paid. What now? I wasn't famous. I had a small radio gig on Central London Radio at the YMCA. Twice a week, I had the afternoon slot called Fresh Air. It was fun but there was no money. I thought I was good, but was I? I was certainly a natural when it came to the musicality of DJ'ing, I never timed intros, I always instinctively knew when the vocals were coming in. Having no full-time gig was a worry. I remember resisting working for Julian Posner at Banana Split, as that's what all the others did. I thought I was better than that. Posner used to call me "Stevie K The Best DJ in the whole UK". There was more than my ego at stake with asking Posner for gigs, as there was no way I was *schlepping* (humping the gear). After years of doing so, my back was shot, I had a hernia operation when I was 17 from schlepping… so no more. So I called Julian and he asked me to come in and have a chat. He knew I was good, but he wasn't prepared for our negotiation. His DJs got paid £50 a gig including the schlepp; I wanted £150 and no schlepping. I remember his reaction; a VERY loud screaming laugh and, "FUCK OFF, who do you think you are?" "Think about it," I said. "You charge £350 normally, plus extras per gig; give me £150, pay for an extra schlepper and sell me in as the premium offer at £750. You'll get more money and I'll get what I want."

He then went full-on Posner – silence, he does this when he's thinking. There have been times over the years when on the phone with me that I thought he had died whilst he was thinking. Anyway, he agreed and despite us meeting many years earlier at Scouts, so began one of the most important relationships of my life and I was a Banana Split DJ. It worked, he sold me in easily; problem was the other DJs caught wind of our deal and they wanted the same. He told them to fuck off too, so they did.

Chapter 7

Video Killed the Radio Star

The Buggles

So I was gigging again, which was good, but I didn't have a proper full-time job – what the hell, I didn't want one. This was all I loved. Music and video. Thanks to the years VJ'ing, my knowledge of the pop video was extensive. Then I saw an ad in Music Week, the trade paper; it was for a company called Diamond Time. It seemed they made music video compilations. One of their brands was called DiscEyes which I had used at the Video Cafe, but this ad was for an office job as a production assistant. I told my Mum and she convinced me to at least go to the interview.

The offices were in super cool Primrose Hill and I remember the boss, Martin Davies, kept me waiting for ages in reception for the interview. To my amazement, he offered me the job, but I wasn't sure. I went home and told my folks that I really didn't think I was suited to an office job even if it was in the music business. Mum said, "Just try it, you never know." I also knew there were over 35,000 DJs in the UK and I needed to be in the top five to make the kind of dough I wanted to make. I accepted the job and stayed with the company for nearly ten years.

During my first few weeks, I was in an office with Michelle and Bella; they were the main producers of the programmes and I was a 'piss-ant' production assistant, writing out cue sheets, stapling and other shit admin work. I knew I needed to be patient, as frankly I knew more about the charts and music than these two, but I got so, so frustrated. One day, I had my silver-tipped cowboy boots on and had to go out to the yard simply to kick holes in all the rubbish bags out of frustration. What the fuck was I doing? I was supposed to be a famous DJ by now. I had all these great clothes and I was working in a fucking office! I consoled myself that I was still a DJ and this was just a day job and it was in the business. I remember there was a tiny rehearsal space in the backyard at Diamond Time and one day I ventured down there as I heard some cool tunes emanating. It turned out to be Curiosity Killed the Cat, one of my favourite bands and a band I had gotten to know a bit at The Video Cafe; that felt cool and we hung out a bit more.

Then something amazing happened: within weeks of each other, both Bella and Michelle left Diamond Time and I was a department of one. If there was no one else then I was the Head of the Department, brilliant. Maybe not, I now had to do all the work by myself, so I thought I would give it a go. The job was straightforward; I had to make the programmes that went into nightclubs, video bars and video jukeboxes all over the bloody world. I had to study the charts for each territory, work out what tunes would work, programme, request clearances from the relevant record companies, then go into the edit suite and trim each track to fit the time-coded windows and in the case of DiscEyes, mix them together in the right order that would work for DJs. I had to be the most qualified person on earth for this gig. I was. I bloody loved it, except for the admin.

Within weeks, I petitioned for an assistant and got one. I wanted to do the licensing myself, to learn, and I was quick to learn. I figured out which record companies would say yes immediately and which required more guile. In those days, it was all via a telex machine. I dealt with all sorts on a daily basis, including a young Simon Cowell, who ran Fanfare Records almost as a one-man band. I dealt with Tony Smith, who was Phil Collins' and Genesis' manager and a whole host of others. My boss, Martin, had a partner. Bruce had devised the royalty rate and sold it into the record industry, but Bruce was lazy and he happily left all the work to me. At first, there was a more senior executive called Tod, and it was he who went into the edit suite to put the programmes together. Tod was better than that, he was a grown-up businessman; surely I should be on the front line with the music. It didn't take much persuading before Tod let me in. Same for Bruce, as he made DiscEyes every month. In those days, they were using a shitty little suite in Soho, just off Golden Square, called Double Vision. I went down there for my first edit. The rest of my life started that day.

In this pokey little suite with an editor and two giant one-inch tape machines, I knew I had found my home for the rest of my life. It was like DJ'ing but more permanent; I had videos, so it was like VJ'ing but more creative and with a much bigger audience, the world.

Diamond Time made programmes for thousands of sites globally and I seemed to be Head of

Programmes within months of joining. From then on, I asked for a pay rise every year and got it. I had landed in the *schmaltz pot* (more Yiddish) meaning 'a great place', and Martin was a great boss; he left me to it. Upon reflection today, they hit the bloody jackpot with me too. I was a natural, young, enthusiastic, and a good leader (within months I had a team of three) and, whilst I relished in the security of a proper job, they must have relished in the quality of work I was producing and now they were freed up, along with Tod, to grow the business, which they duly did. I was a big part of that company and it felt like we grew every year.

I remember in the early days putting a timesheet together of overtime as that's what Michelle and Bella did. Martin called me in and explained that he understood why I did it but it wasn't appropriate for me as mine wasn't just a job, it was a career. Martin, if you are reading or listening to this, I have been using that line with my staff for the last 25 years, so thank you. Martin and Bruce, my two bosses, were so different. Martin was hard-working, lovely and long-winded, whereas Bruce was lazy, brief, and not so nice (and he smelt). Bruce sat over the record company deals but left me to the day-to-day. He only called me in once every three months when he decided to pay royalties to the record companies and he would ask me who was it important that we paid. I didn't understand; surely if you had a contract and royalties were due, you had to pay them all, no? Apparently not. Bruce very cheekily used the royalty income stream to cash flow the business. To this day, I'm not sure if that was genius or just wrong.

One story I remember well was when I was in an edit suite in St Johns Wood. Godley and Creme, the pop stars from 10cc and now superstar music video directors, were in the suite next door. There was a pungent smell of weed wafting through the air-con. They popped their heads into my suite where I was making Disc Eyes and asked what I was doing. When I told them it was a compilation of the latest videos and they wanted a copy. I replied, "Roll me a joint and I'll get you one." Ten minutes later, they came back with the biggest joint I had ever seen. I drew around it diagonally on an A4 piece of paper; it was about 12 inches long… that was nice of them. I think it took me a week to smoke.

Chapter 8

I'm Moving Out

Billy Joel

So, I had a proper job; I was still DJ'ing on the side with Banana Split and at the age of about 21, Julian Spalter and I decided to buy a flat together. The flat was No.1, The Reddings in Borehamwood. It was £64,000 and we got a mortgage of £32,000 each. I took Mum and Dad's old sofa. We bought a TV. We had avocado green carpet. I took the slightly bigger bedroom ("I'll have way more birds back than you, you moron.") and we were off. I had moved out. More recently, Mum told me that she asked Dad to give me £5,000 to help me on my way when moving out of home. I had been financially independent since I crashed their Mini Metro, so didn't expect anything. I was fiercely independent and wanted to do everything myself and my way. Dad apparently explained to Mum that he wanted me to do it for myself too, and if I ever needed anything, he would be there. Fine by me, as it gave me a work ethic and self-discipline that has never let me down.

Dad was an accountant and had trained me to do my own books every year; I kept all my receipts and invoices. I was on it and determined to have a good life, just as it had begun since I started DJ'ing. I liked having money, it gave me choices, although that wouldn't always be the case.

Julian and I were best mates but living with this idiot was another story. One year, I went to Marbella and spent too much on very expensive clothes in a really cool shop called Gomina. I was friendly with the girl who worked there; she was called Isabelle and I got a small discount. That year, I bought these Bowie balloon-style red trousers, an amazing leather-fronted checked jacket and an incredible Armand Basi T-shirt. I remember coming home from that holiday and opening my Barclaycard bill. It was over £500. "I'm going to kill myself", I told Julian; he creased up. I was a spender, but always confident that with my job and additional income from DJ'ing I could afford it. This felt like a step too far but somehow the bill got paid and I survived.

A few weeks later, I woke up late on Saturday morning. I went into the kitchen to make a cup of tea and there was Spalter, standing there, eating a bowl of corn flakes in his boxers and my fucking Armand Basi T-shirt. I hadn't worn it yet; it was so special and this cunt had worn it to bed that night. I went mad and he found it all very amusing, so amusing that he spat his corn flakes all over my £200 T-shirt, probably the equivalent of £500 today. The next day, I had a locksmith put a lock on my door (the thieving bastard is still one of my best mates today).

After a year or so, Julian announced he was leaving his job in the city and going to study to be a lawyer. I was going to have to take over the mortgage, which I thought I could just about manage, so off he fucked. In those days, we had no forms to sign; we just did it. Today, such a manoeuvre would be impossible.

Julian, despite not living with me, remained a clothes thief. I remember one night going out in this fantastic letterman baseball jacket I had bought in Sweden. My friend Michael's sister, Natalie, approached me and asked me why I was wearing Julian's jacket. Cunt. (Julian, not Natalie.)

So now I was living alone, which proved to be

amazing. I had this pulling technique… I still was an avid concertgoer, I went to everything and I always bought two tickets. A few days before the gig, I would approach any girl I fancied and ask if they fancied going to see Duran Duran, or whoever that week. Easy. The answer was usually a yes.

Talking about Duran reminds me of the time when I took my good friend, Michael (my Video Cafe assistant), to the Rio tour at Hammersmith Odeon. Michael was a couple of years younger than me, so I picked him up and drove there and back. When we got home, we were going up to his room to check out something, I'm not sure what. As he put his key in the door, his mum opened it in her flesh-coloured bra and knickers; she was waiting up for her young son, 'worried sick'. She immediately tried to cover herself up but only had her arms to do so. "Oh my God, Michael!" she screamed. For about the next 20 years, whenever I saw Michael's mum, I always said, "I didn't recognise you with your clothes on." It always made us laugh.

Michael and I became the best of friends, and along with Julian and our other friends, Simon and another Michael, became a gang of five that still remains today.

One night at that time, at the Hippodrome, I had been seeing this pretty girl with a mass of curly hair called Samantha only for a week or so, almost a record for me. I arrived late and saw her in the area where we usually all congregated; her mouth was firmly open and clamped over another boy's mouth called Sammy. For some reason, I thought it was a good idea to tap them both on the shoulder and smack Sammy as hard as I could in the face. Sammy was a legendary tough nut in every sense of both words. He didn't flinch and whacked me back a lot harder. I saw stars, Samantha screamed, everybody piled in to break it up and that was it for me and Sam. Sam went on to marry my best mate, Michael, and they are both amongst my very best friends today, but they had to suffer me calling Sam one of my cast-offs for quite a few years. This is still a great story; for some reason, Sam doesn't agree.

So I was settled in a good job at Diamond Time that I really enjoyed. I had decided that my ambition to be a famous DJ was wobbling. There were 35,000 DJs in the UK and I figured only about five, who had made it onto TV, were worth what I wanted to be worth, not just financially but generally, 5–35,000 was too big of a gap and in my head I thought I might not want this challenge anymore; the odds weren't stacked in my favour at all. This was all well before the notion of superstar DJs that eventually came along several years later after House Music really took off.

Meanwhile the set up at Diamond Time was developing; I had assistants and built things up nicely for myself there. As part of my weekly routine, I was liaising with record companies on a daily basis. I remember going to a meeting at Island Records with their then MD Marc Marrott; his desk was huge and completely empty, bar a couple of cassettes. How cool was that? Mine was piled high with files; I wanted a big empty desk but figured I'd have to wait a bit. I never did achieve this small ambition as my desk was always full of files…

At this time, I took on a side project managing a band of mates who were in a great rock band called Protocol. I thought I could help, I couldn't really; they were seriously good and had some fantastic songs. I made a video for them and then they disbanded. My short spell in management only stretched out again to a female DJ called Wendy Lloyd. I had hired Wendy to present a rock show I was making for ITV called *Thargs Rock Power*. Jonathan Glazer directed it, yes, THAT Jonathan Glazer. We were mates back then and I've just seen his masterpiece *Zone of Interest* and will never forget *Sexy Beast*. Back to Wendy, I thought she was very good so I offered to manage her as well, she said yes and I proceeded to get her a gig on Radio 1, the biggest radio station in the country back then. She turned the gig down and went to Virgin which had just launched. I told her it was not the right decision but she fired me and went with a very successful radio manager who happened to be a good friend of mine. When I called him to tell him my story he had no idea of the background and promptly fired her. So did Virgin. Shame (not). That was me trying out management and it was a clear lesson to avoid it at all costs from thereon in.

Also at this time, I became friendly with a bunch of the folk that worked in the music business, particularly at CBS (now Sony); they were located in Soho Square. My mate, Steve, made all the pop videos, Sarah was in the promo department and there was this nice guy called Rob who was in marketing. Rob was Rob Stringer who now runs Sony worldwide. What a success story he was. I hope he writes a book one day. This gang often met in the bar in the basement of their office and I hung with them.

One night, we all went out for dinner and there was a girl sitting opposite me called Belinda. I was flirting with her but she was on a date with some rich dude. As we left, I put my card in her palm, which she promptly screwed up and threw to the floor. Oh well, no biggie. Evidently she went home to her flatmates', Sarah and Helen and their friend Michele who went on to run a huge rock 'n' roll limo service and Helen is a world-renowned tour manager today. Anyway, back to the point, these girls were more interested in what I was about than Belinda and they convinced her to call me to find out more.

During that period, I had a music membership to a nightclub in town called Browns. It was completely different to the clubs I had worked in; for a start, it was a lot smaller. It had an upstairs VIP section which I sometimes blagged my way into and George Michael was often there. It seems Belinda had been down there a short while before and 'checked me out', all I did was dance and drink water. I was still gigging and a few months earlier, Andrew Ridgeley's two naughty best mates, John and Dave, hired me to DJ a new club night they wanted to run in Rickmansworth called Vertigo; sounded good to me.

There I was on opening night, with the 'it' crowd again, some rough locals and a few of my friends. It was the very early nineties and one of the 'it' crowd offered me an E. I'd never heard of them; they were very new to the scene, apparently not addictive and had no side effects. So I took it and, in true Kemsley style, only took half of this tiny pill. OMG! It was bloody fantastic, so for almost a year, from that night on, I took half an E on a Friday night at Browns and half on a Saturday. One night, going home alone at about 3 am, I decided to drive straight over a green filter left turn light, inadvertently jumping a red light. I was hungry and fancied a bagel from Carmelies in Golden Green (it's still there today). I saw a police van in my rear mirror and, still a little hyper from my half an E, I thought it would be a good idea to take a left and try and lose them. Cue blue lights and a pull over in the side street. "You weren't trying to get away from us were you, sir?" About four of them searched my car, they searched my pockets, they looked at my banknotes (for traces of cocaine I guessed), had a good look at me and let me go. Es were so new that the police hadn't even heard of them yet; this was about two years before "the summer of love and raves". I had the other half of the pill in the bullet pocket of my 501s; it was so small that there was no way they could find it, and the only clue whether someone had taken one of these pills was dilated pupils. The police simply didn't know that then. I've been getting away with it (all my life).

Another night, my buddy John and I both popped half an E before driving up to Browns. As we left The Reddings, where I lived, we both swear a traffic cone moved across the whole road by itself. It wasn't windy, we pulled over and the cone was weighted and bloody heavy; to this day an unexplained phenomenon. Probably the drugs…. I stopped taking Es less than a year after I started. It was fun, but people were now taking too many at raves and I'm not an addictive person, so one day I thought I'd stop and simply did.

Back to Belinda. Well, a week or so later, Belinda did call and I arranged to meet her at Double Vision Studios in Newman Street, W1. I was in a huge studio with lots of TVs and music etc; I hoped she'd be impressed. She wasn't. We went out to a friend's dinner and had a snog in the cab on the way to drop her home. She was nice, pretty, and had a really friendly, disarming personality and, yes, you guessed it, she was older; six years older than me. She was also, gasp, shock, horror – Jewish. I never really dated Jewish girls, I thought they were usually a pain in the ass and so immature, but Belinda was different – I was 24, she was 30. She dressed nicely and had a slight Mancunian accent – interesting. We arranged to meet that weekend for a date, I think it was Hyde

Park, Pizza Hut and the cinema. In the middle of that date, we ended up at her place and one thing led to another, as it tended to in those days. The only reason that I mention this, is that right in the middle of our bedroom activity, and I mean right in the middle, the phone went. The answer machine clicked on and we paused. "Belinda", came this Mancunian-accented older lady, "Mummy here, call me please." Lila, my mother-in-law-to-be, interrupted our first intimate moment.

As I write this today, my eyes are tearing up. Lila recently passed away and I loved her so much, she was the most wonderful mother-in-law any boy could wish for. Anyway, I digress. The date continued and I think I ended up staying the night. From that night onwards, I'm not sure we had many apart (unless I was away working abroad later in life). For our second date, we went with some friends to see Paul McKenna the hypnotist and I was hypnotised on stage to be Elvis Presley singing into a broomstick and dancing every time *Jailhouse Rock* came on. There were about 2,000 people in that theatre, but hypnotism removes inhibitions. My friend, Paul, was being a dick that night and it was embarrassing, so I called Belinda later to apologise and say that it wasn't me but him who was the immature one. She later said that she was going to end it with me as Paul's dicking around showed her that the age gap might be a problem.

It didn't help that the first night she came back to my flat, Julian had left a message on my answering machine. I duly pressed play as we entered the living room. Beep. "May the flies of a thousand camels infest your arse and give you gonorrhoea, call me," was the message. "Who was that?" Belinda said, not sure what to make of it. "It's my best mate, Julian; he used to live here," came the weak response. The age difference however never was a problem for us. I was always mature beyond my years and it turned out that Belinda was immature for her age, so I guess we met in the middle. Belinda was having an affair with her then-boss when we met and he was minted, but she dumped him for me, who wasn't.

There was a funny night in that flat that I have to tell you about. It was Boxing Day and my friends were over playing Trivial Pursuit – Michael, Julian, Simon and, of course, me and Belinda. We went to bed early and left them to it. The next morning, I woke to find the TV in the kitchen. What the fuck? Then I saw the sofa was where the table and chairs used to be and the table and chairs where the TV used to be. The wankers had silently completely shuffled my entire flat around. It was funny, but then I saw an opportunity to exact my revenge. Julian had left his brand new trendy Filofax in my flat. It was a medium-sized Filofax with all his calendar set up for the next year and more importantly all his many names and addresses filed alphabetically. Not anymore. I shuffled everything into an unrecognisable order. Touché.

I specifically remember asking myself one day, what was I doing with this lady? She really wasn't my obvious type, but she was fun and made me look good with her outgoing personality. She moved out of her Maida Vale flat-share and into mine and in less than a year, I was in Manchester asking Lila for Belinda's hand in marriage. "You're mad," Lila spat. "You've no idea what you're letting yourself in for." So I went to her brother, David, who was studying for his law finals. "Piss off, you idiot," he retorted, then I went to her older brother, Simon. "You're a bloody twat. You've no idea, have you?" I ignored them all.

I do remember thinking, how can I afford a diamond ring? I had friends in the diamond business back then and I got some samples of what I thought I could afford. Now you remember my Dad didn't give me the £5k my Mum asked him to give; well, it turned out he had bought some new issue BT shares in my name at about that time. I needed the dough for an engagement ring, so he told me about the shares. We cashed them in for about five grand, sorted. This sort of thing has happened to me all my life. When I had a big unexpected tax bill, I got a rebate; when I needed to sell a house or flat in the future, a buyer popped out of nowhere. I've been getting away with it (all my life). I bought a selection of diamonds home and laid them out, proud as punch that I was able to do this. "They're all a bit small," said my intended, I kid you not. So we went down in quality and up in size. No biggie, I thought. We were married just over a year after we met. Only the second girl I'd ever been out with really.

Once Belinda had moved into my flat in Borehamwood, she started to meet all my friends, and as we all grew together, she got friendly with the girlfriends and then wives, who were all considerably younger than she was. It didn't seem to matter and we all blended well. We married in May 1991, I was happy. Our first dance was *Father Figure*; Belinda had lost her dad soon after her first marriage was failing, and he was such a key figure in her life. I guess I was looking to help replace that mature guiding type and thought I could be her father figure. In hindsight, probably not the right move, but what did I know? I was 26!

Chapter 9

Adult Education
Hall & Oats

We moved to a very small flat in Hendon; it was our first marital home. Belinda worked as a PA and I was at Diamond Time, supplementing my income with DJ'ing. Life felt good. My single friends still hung and Belinda liked them all and was happy for us to all watch football together (which we still do today). Then, in September 1992, Black Wednesday happened; the economy took a sharp turn for the worse and interest rates rocketed to over 15%! I had a variable mortgage. FUCK! My mortgage payments alone were now more than I earned. I think I got a tiny sympathetic raise but I was going to have to DJ more. The other Julian at Banana Split was able to give me more work; his business was growing and growing and he was now a bonafide event planner with several mobile discos on the road. He also did balloons and supplied party poppers etc. He always went the extra mile. It was impressive, but not nearly as impressive as where he ultimately took the business later in life. Frankly, if it wasn't for DJ'ing, we would have lost that flat. We got through it. Belinda didn't complain even when one week I stated, "It's beans on toast every day this week." Quite simply, when you are young, the fall to the ground doesn't seem as painful as you think it is when you are older.

Belinda's biological clock was ticking and talk of babies began. In the midst of this economic slump, it didn't seem the best idea, but I said, "Sure, why not?" Again, lack of fear in the young mind. Amazingly, neither of us had a clue about ovulation and all that stuff and for over two years nothing happened. We didn't panic and were both seemingly relaxed. We even talked of adoption should it not be able to happen for us. We both had tests and both seemed ok. One day, Belinda's friend, Mandy, who very sadly was in hospital with cancer with no hope of survival, insisted that Belinda went to see her brother, Richard, who was a gynaecologist; Belinda made a promise to Mandy that she would. Before we went to see Richard, we had a trip to Israel planned. I had never been to Israel. The trip was amazing. It was actually the result of me winning a golf competition called the Israeli Cup and it was paid for! It was also a revelation for me. I'd never felt particularly close to Judaism but going to Israel was special. I found it strange that all these people were Jewish. I know that sounds weird, but I was secular, and although a lot of our friends were Jewish, it was never a big deal for me. Israel felt special and I won the bloody international competition out there as well. I received my prize from Chaim Herzog who was the President of Israel; imagine that! We saw the sights, the Dead Sea, Mount Sinai and of course went to Jerusalem. At the Wailing Wall, so named as people prayed there so intensely they wailed, Belinda, as tradition dictates, wrote a prayer and placed it in the cracks of this, the holiest site in all of Judaism. It said that if God gave her a baby and it was a boy, she would Barmitzvah him at the wall. Typical Belinda, setting sights and expenditure levels high! I didn't complain.

When we returned from Israel, we went to see Richard the gynaecologist. He said he just needed to do a simple "scrape out", his words, not mine, and all should be well. He did and it was. On the 8th of April 1994, Joseph Frank Kemsley entered the world by C-section. When electing for a C-section, Belinda joked to Richard, "Just knock me out and wake me up when the hairdresser is there." As an aside, Joe was called Frankie for about five days until our sister-in-law, Tina, said it sounded like he was a pizza man. Never afraid of speaking her mind was our Tina.

Sleepless nights ensued. I was working hard to make ends meet and having struggled for so long to conceive, didn't give a moment's thought to a second pregnancy. 13 months later, Louis Sam Kemsley arrived, screaming, as he tended to do for the next year, the little fucker!

Two babies under 13 months was fucking hard. Belinda, in my view, definitely had some postnatal depression after Louis, but that wasn't really known about or even talked about in those days. Diamond Times business was picking up pace and I often felt as if I was about to start my second job as a husband and father when driving home from work in those days. We had managed to move to a tiny "two-up, two-down" detached house in Edgware. It's a long story that I won't bore you with, but I ended up threatening to sue Barrett Homes over sound transference in our first flat. Every night there, we could hear the two girls who lived upstairs peeing. I'm a light sleeper, so one of them, who pissed like a horse, woke me up every night. One of those girls and her then-boyfriend became our best couple friends and they still are great friends today. We went on many holidays together over many years. All from going to the toilet! Barrett Homes agreed to re-house us and I managed to port my mortgage over with the house move – Lord knows how – and we continued to just about survive financially by the skin of our teeth. Business however was looking up.

Chapter 10

Banana Republic

Boomtown Rats

During this time of trying to make babies and eventually succeeding, two quite unique occurrences happened in my work life. As I said earlier, I was doing well at Diamond Time and was able to convince my bosses I should be able to produce some additional videos like karaoke videos; these required more creativity and, in some cases, shooting. This was a buzz and I started to learn about matters outside of licensing and the edit suite I so loved. I began creating income for the business. My boss, Martin, was always saying I could get a percentage of the business one day but the most I got in terms of confirmation was a handwritten note on a shorthand pad.

One day, on my insistence, we went to see Diamond Time's lawyers. I took my sister-in-law, Shelley Ann, who was a lawyer. After the meet, Shelley and I got into a tiny lift and she told me that I would never get what I wanted from "that man". I knew she was right; I'd known for some time, but hearing it from Shelley bought it home.

The following week, I started telling a very select group of potential partners that I wanted to go out on my own. By this time, I had Top Shop as a client and I knew they'd follow me anywhere, as I had been doing some great work for them which included promos shot on film, cool sizzles and filming their fashion shows. I also knew I wouldn't 'nick' and didn't want Diamond Time's core business, which was the music video compilations. I had the bug for real video and film production and I wanted to be more creative now; I knew I had the skill set and determination to go for it. In hindsight, it was a mental time to jump from a good, safe job. I was in my early thirties and we had two babies. WTAF? I had three meetings with three potential partners and I offered them all the same deal – 50% of my business if they covered my £40,000 salary, all business overheads and my two cars. What a deal for them that would turn out to be; no wonder all three said yes.

I went, without hesitation, with my friend Julian Posner at Banana Split; firstly, because we were friends, secondly, I loved the name and thought Banana Split Video Productions sounded good, and thirdly, he had a great phone number – (8) 200 1234 – and lastly, I thought I could get the new company and new logo on all his vans that were in London all the time and my potential clients, who were so different to Julian's, would think I had a big shoot going on at a posh hotel.

Less than two weeks after that lawyer's meeting with Martin, I shook hands with Julian and agreed to go for it. An interesting point to make is that Julian and I ran the business for nearly six years on a handshake and never had an argument or disagreement. I told Belinda, she had helped me type up a business plan. I handed my notice in at Diamond Time and I remember feeling a bit hurt that they didn't try to stop me from leaving. Within four weeks, I had a desk, a phone and one client. Within one year, we had four desks, an edit suite and three staff. Whey-hey! Unbeknownst to Julian and me, his clientele was about to change to include some super-wealthy individuals, in particular, an Arab Prince.

I had just gone out on my own in business. Belinda

spotted a house in Uphill Road, Mill Hill in the paper; it was a small house but bigger than where we were and Uphill was the best road in the area by some way. I didn't know how I was going to afford it but Belinda had assured me that if we bought this house, she would never ask me for another thing – ever!

About this time, a good friend of mine, Michael Crooke, one of my gang who was a partner of Julian's at the time, was asked to DJ at Wembley Stadium. He said he couldn't do it (I have never understood why – Mike?) but recommended me for the gig. Would I do it? Fuck yeah! Our eldest, Joe had just been born and I went along to DJ at the FA Cup Semi Finals of 1994 that were being held at the world-famous Wembley Stadium for the first time. One of the four teams was mine, Manchester United. What a buzz. There was already some posh bloke doing the announcements but I was to save the FA about £15,000 on a marching band by playing my records instead.

I talked on the mic between tracks and handed over to the posh announcer to do the teams and official announcements. By the time the Final was upon us, out went the posh bloke and in came me! I was given carte blanche to do as I saw fit with the music and make all the announcements as well. It was an incredible gig and at that point I had no idea how long it would last. It ended up being the start of an incredible 15-year stint working for the FA, not just at Wembley but all over Europe. More about this in a bit....

Enter Phil Street. Phil was my bank manager at Barclays in Harrow on the Hill, where I had been since I was about 14 years old. Phil came to see me at Banana and at that point we had 36 invoices. We had traded for less than one year and I needed a 100% mortgage to get the house of our dreams. Phil was about 19 years old, I offered him two tickets to a Wembley match and he said, "Ok, sign here." It really was that easy, which is incredible to think about, bearing in mind what young people have to go through today to get a mortgage. Our accountant at the time, Leo, said I was mad and had "balls the size of dump trucks," but the truth was that the risk just didn't register. I was young and I have always likened this period in my life to being like a six-year-old skier, bombing down the mountain with no fear. What does a six-year-old understand about the risks of going that fast? What did I understand? Posner was fully supportive; he knew I would have to work my bollocks off to make the business a success and to pay the mortgage. Shrewd man. It would certainly up the value of his shares. I did work fucking hard and I never missed a mortgage payment, ever. The family was growing older and the business started to grow as well.

As I just mentioned, there was this insanely wealthy Arab Prince who had asked Julian to make him a series of parties. Julian and his designer, Wolter, drew up plans and Julian and I decided to go to Paris to meet the Prince at The George V hotel with the idea that I would pitch to film the parties as they were to have live acts and I could shoot them like concerts. Off on the Euro Star we went for our 4pm rendezvous.

We arrived in good time, having gotten up early in London, and we were sat outside the Prince's suite by 3.30pm. We remained there like two naughty boys outside the headmaster's office for the next six hours and then the Prince emerged. Six fucking hours waiting. In we went, and the Prince instantly asked before starting if it was Julian who also created parties for a certain Sultan. Julian explained that client confidentiality was paramount to him. The Prince asked him again and again, but Julian refused to comment. Then the Prince said, "If you did the Sultan's parties, you can do mine." "Yes, your

Highness, that was me," he spluttered out, forgetting his principles. The Prince looked at the plans and told Julian he wanted the A party for the C price. Of course he did. A deal was agreed and then it was my turn. I pitched for about £50,000 to film everything with multiple cameras, more than I had ever charged for anything at that time and he just said to me, "Do it." Fuck! I could have got £100k easily, fuck….

He then stated to us both, "Come, we walk!" What? Julian and I were knackered; we'd been up since 6am – it was now 10.30pm. We'd missed our train home and now we had to go on a walk! "Of course, we'd love to," Julian chirped. Off we went down the Champs-Élysées with a Royal Prince and his entourage, including a jester (I kid you not), a hairdresser, a doctor, various secretaries and the Prince's children. After an hour of walking, with Julian and I staying slightly behind the group, the Prince decided he wanted to go to the cinema to watch *The Hunt for Red October*, we had to follow….

When inside the cinema, the Prince's aides offered each person already in there a €500 note to leave the cinema to make it a private screening. Julian and I sat at the back not quite understanding what on earth we were doing there whilst Sean Connery was saving submarines. We got back to the hotel, starving hungry and exhausted but we had won the work. It was the most bizarre pitch either of us had ever been involved in and, to this day, it has not been surpassed in weirdness.

That summer, it was time for the agreed jobs to take place; we were to shoot in Cannes followed later by Disneyland Paris. The first job was mental. We were set up by 9pm, having arrived in France that morning, and then we did that waiting thing again. I had three cameras and a de-rig mixing station. I was going to cut the gigs live. A rumour started circulating that Michael Jackson was going to be a guest at the party. The main act that night was Patti La Belle.

Julian and I, together with one of my cameramen, waited at the top of the steps of the famous Palais De Festival and at about midnight, a group of people carriers drove up on the pavement and out emerged our Prince and Michael fucking Jackson! You have to understand that "Jacko" was by some distance the biggest star in the world and here he was at my first-ever multi-camera shoot. He was dressed in the full get up: epaulettes, trilby hat and the military-style jacket. The crowds immediately gathered around the bottom of the steps at the Palais De Festival and the

King of Pop and our Prince made their escape up those red carpeted steps. A little wave from Michael back to the crowd and the rumours were proved true. I can assure you to this day neither of us were convinced until it actually happened that they were true.

A number of Arabic superstars performed. The Prince asked to see me; he called me "director" and asked me if the artists' clothes were ok on the backdrop. I looked through my fingers like a real director and assured him it was all perfect. Patti La Belle then came on and she was amazing and THEN she asked Michael to come up on stage. The crowd went nuts; when I say crowd, there were about 30 guests! Michael went up and did the full Michael Jackson thing, spinning, dancing, whooping and making those noises he used to make. Julian ran up to me and shouted, "Are you getting this?" – "No," I remarked sarcastically, "I've stopped."

We had been in France since 9 am and the next morning at 9 am, Julian and I walked back to The Carlton Hotel from The Palais in a daze, dressed in our smart 'blacks' whilst everyone else was arriving at the beach in their swimwear. We were silent, exhausted and bewildered.

A few weeks later, we did Disneyland featuring Shanice, who had just had a worldwide No.1 with *I love your Smile*, and MC Hammer. They shut down the park and our Prince went on Space Mountain with his crew. I filmed every second of these mad parties and will never forget them. Julian and I went on to create these special concert parties and film them for a few more years: on the Prince's boat, in Los Angeles at The Beverly Wilshire Hotel and all over the world. In the end, he bought the Arabic equivalent of MTV and I was out of there… What a run it was though and what a way to cut my teeth as a concert director. We produced over 100 hours of material and were able to establish the business financially and technically with our first ever on-line edit suite.

Talking of technical, there was a lesson learnt during that period. When I did get back to London from France, we started the editing process immediately, but there was a problem. There was a white sash line on all the footage and I had no idea why. It was my first ever multi-cam shoot and these lines made our lovely footage look like it was shot on VHS rather than professional broadcast cameras. What transpired is that the cables from our cameras had been sitting on the lighting cables for the show, and in those days, they were not protected in the same way they are today, and the electric current showed up on every second of my footage, there was over 150 hours' worth.

I decided to edit anyway so there would be less hours to fix and then, purely by luck, I found some new technology called "Chop 'em out". There was no internet to rely on to try and find this technology and it was so new that they had never dealt with this issue before. I paid the exorbitant costs as we simply couldn't afford to mess this up and we got it fixed (I've been getting away with it, all my life). To this day. it still feels like a miracle.

Part of the plan in those early days was television production; I wasn't sure in what guise but it was a market and we were a production company. A school friend and experienced documentary producer and his partner contacted me about an idea called *The Left Hand of Tantra*. There had recently been a 16-page article in the Sunday Times Magazine about child sacrifice in India, and next year was to be India's 50th anniversary of its independence. David and Arun were convinced this would be unique and we would get the story – they would both fly out to India for a month to further investigate and shoot. I liked it but I wasn't prepared to fund it fully. We were a fledgling business, doing well but just starting.

That spring, I went out to the TV market in Cannes and somehow got a meeting with both the chairman and MD of Yorkshire TV, the legendary Bruce Gingall and David Holdgate. I told them passionately about the idea and they too thought it could be an important documentary. The problem was that David and Arun wanted to fly out in the next week to cover an important ceremony called Kali Puga with a highly respected priest. Bruce and David told me to get the flight costs covered by their Head of Documentaries. This knob spent days avoiding me, clearly pissed off that his bosses were telling him what to make and not make and would not commit. I had to decide whether to go for it or not. I did, and off Arun and David went. In fairness to them, they absolutely came back with film confirmation of a very real, scary and difficult story proving that child sacrifice was happening in rural India with full witness and police interviews on camera.

In the interim, this Chris, Head of Documentaries, poured scorn on the whole idea and doubted its validity. I told him about the Sunday Times article and that I had already paid for the flights and the shoot was going well, but he was rude and dismissive. We finished the film which cost over £80k, and in order to try and get my money back, I thought I would try and sell it myself at the next market. This was the worst mistake I made in those days… stick to what you know Kemsley; I'm not a distributor or a salesman. I got VERY close with Channel 4 *Dispatches* but ultimately, the subject matter was deemed too politicly sensitive at the time. The film has never been seen or aired anywhere, which is a real shame. It really hurt me financially, but a lesson was learnt.

I went to the markets in Cannes between 1992 until I finally couldn't take the walking, talking and the general grind some 25 years later. Cannes has a life of it's own in my memory, from a flight home in a hurricane where we either thought we were going to die or just throw up (I was in the later section) to important, worth while meetings, starting relationships that lasted a lifetime in business and life.

Chapter 11

For Your Babies

Simply Red

We had two young sons under the age of two and there was a lot going on. I remember Louis, our second child, he was a crier. We'd already gone through the sleepless nights with Joe, including sitting downstairs on that awful night when we left him crying in his cot for what seemed like an hour – in reality, it was a lot less. At last, Joe fell asleep, and was finally able to sleep through the night after that. Now here came Louis, who was even worse. He was always bloody hungry and one night feed I will never forget was after he drained nine ounces of milk at 3 am then just wailed. "Shut up, shut the fuck up," I found myself saying with my hands nearly around his neck. Everyone else was fast asleep and I just didn't want them to be woken up. I caught myself but it was scary and it showed me the reality of sleep depravation and the real pressures parenthood can bring at this stage of life.

Louis also decided one day to choke on a tiny button or coin he'd found in the corner somewhere. He went purple and blue. I thought he was going to die. This incident was so traumatic that to this day, Belinda and I can't agree on who actually picked him up like a 'little piggy going to market' and ran down the stairs with him until he coughed it up. I swear I did the stair run, my ex disagrees. I'm happy to report that Louis is the most chilled of all our kids today, and he is nearly 30 now.

Joe, the big boy at nearly two, just didn't eat anything other than chicken nuggets or those Petits Filous baby yoghurts for years. A paediatrician at the time assured us that no Jewish child had et died of malnutrition in North West London. Today, he'll eat anything and is a real foodie. Back then, I also remember one day, he jumped out of my arms head first into what was effectively a concrete floor. "What was that noise?" came the shout from the kitchen. "Joe's head on the floor," I replied, just before that delayed reaction of screaming began. It ain't straightforward having kids and, as they say, there is no manual; you have to trust your instincts; they are nearly always right (particularly a mother's instinct).

I think this period was the second toughest of my life, that second job as I approached the door at home thing. When I returned from the Michael Jackson gig in Cannes, Belinda opened the front with Louis in her arms and promptly shut it on my beaming face. I was buzzing from the work and she simply didn't need to see that at this particular moment in time. I'm not sure if Belinda agrees today, but as I said earlier, it is my absolute belief that she had a period of postnatal depression. We didn't know much about this phenomenon at the time, but I found myself in the back garden that summer on the phone to my mother-in-law, Lila, telling her that I wasn't sure if I could do this anymore. Lila was her usual pragmatic, glorious self, and we kept calm and carried on.

I was driven. I was in my early thirties and I thought this was the one opportunity I would have to really make a go of it. I had to graft, and graft hard. I also had to be the best dad and husband that I could be. It was clear that to play golf on the weekend for five hours was unreasonable, so I stopped that (for nine years) to apply myself to the three major tasks at hand. In fairness to Belinda, she never stopped me from working or moaned about the hours that I sometimes had to keep. She knew what I was trying to do and that her and our boys were my main focus for these ambitions. I wanted the good life and I knew I was going to have to work hard and clever to achieve it, but at least I was blessed with doing something that I mostly loved.

My first ever feature-length sell-through video shoot was called *Babies at Play* and it was just that. Sell-through video were the VHSs and later DVDs that you could buy in the shops, like Woolies, WHSmith and HMV. There was a hit video in America and we just copied it; it starred a one and two-year-old Joe and Louis and my nephew Daniel, plus a bunch of other babies. It was great and was a minor hit. My first full-length sell-through video produced, another 200 or so to go… during that period, kids' videos became a thing for me at Banana Split. I made loads including *Learn and Play the Montessori Way*, *Tumble Tots* and lots more. The talent was cheap as all our friends wanted their kids in my videos, and frankly, I was good with kids. Easy win and a good start to a career in sell-through video.

Around that time, Nikki joined my fledgling business. Nikki was my first ever producer and she and I drove all the work. I would centre on capturing the work, she would produce and I would direct. We were an awesome team. She told me a few years later that when she came to the interview, she went home and spoke to her husband and said that she thought the business was cool, but she wasn't sure about the guy (me). Well up until I recently sold my third business, Nikki continued to work for me. I say work for me, because for the first 15 years, it was very much with me and in the last 11, more for me as she took over from me as the businesses grew, and became a better (creative) director than I was.

She recently recounted a story about those early days when we would drive around together going to meetings in town. Whilst driving around town, I was always on the car phone. By then, I had upgraded to a Range Rover, something that Julian, my business partner, very much encouraged (he knew I'd have to work hard to keep up the payments) The car had an early version of a speech recognition car phone and Nikki was in regular hysterics when it didn't recognise what I was saying, and I would swear and curse at the fucking thing whilst Nikki pissed herself. Nikki remembered that in between calls and meetings, Belinda called and asked me to cancel a nail appointment; apparently, I said ok and did it. Nikki was flabbergasted; she knew how hard I was working, why would I agree to do this menial task? I guess I felt, as the saying goes, 'happy wife, happy life'. Nik is convinced it's a Jewish culture thing and I think she's probably right.

The work got better and better; we were making great trailers for home video and cinema releases, working with cool clients and making a profit. My lifestyle was getting better. It seemed Posner may have backed a winner.

Chapter 12

Three Lions on a Shirt

The Lightning Seeds

It was now 1996, not a year I will ever forget. I was firmly established as the DJ and the "Voice of Wembley"; the atmosphere was greatly improved from those days of marching bands. I did all the England home games, all the football finals between the Twin Towers and I got paid! I even got given two tickets to every match or gig for my friends and family. I had an unbelievable parking space right outside the Royal Tunnel, and now that CDs were a thing, I didn't have to schlep my heavy record cases; all I had was a couple of books of CDs.

To be honest with you, my Wembley and beyond stories are a book on their own; I simply haven't got the 'cha-chick' to mention them all here. I had already experienced my 15 seconds of fame at my first-ever FA Cup Final; back then, my seat was on the back row of the England bench and the Royal line-up was done in double-quick time. The Cup Final had a television audience of over a billion people in those days. I had done my thing, announcing the teams, the anthems etc and United were ready to kick off against Chelsea. The BBC commentator was talking about Andy Cole, who had recently signed for United from Newcastle, and he was 'cup-tied' so couldn't play. Andy was sat directly in front of me in his Cup Final suit and as the camera zoomed in on him, he decided to tie his shoelaces. I had a TV to help me with the substitutions and goal scorers and as I glanced at it, there I was. It was 15 seconds before the kick-off, full screen. Andy must have decided to do the other lace up whilst he was down there as the director kept on the shot for at least eight seconds and my Papa Issy was heard shouting at the TV, "Look, there's Steven, there's Steven." It was the classic 15 (minutes), in my case, seconds of fame and for the next week, loads of people commented how they saw me on the 'telly' at the Cup Final.

Back to Euro 96. The European Championships took everything to another level. I was asked to programme all the music for all the other DJs in the different stadiums up and down the country. I knew what worked, what was cool at that time, and I relished the job and duly sent out CDs and back-up CDs to all the announcers. I was also asked because of my work within the music business if I could book singers for the quarter-finals onwards to sing the national anthem. Now, here's the thing, officially Wembley Stadium was not an England home game. So what happened to change the mood at the FA and, in my opinion, bend the official UEFA ruling? It was a sunny Saturday; it was England's second game at Wembley against "the old enemy" Scotland. The Scottish fans were in fine voice. I remember playing *Rocking All Over the World* at half-time and the Scots went mental, they sang it so loud, much to the amusement of the England fans. Cue the second half: Terry Venables bought on Jamie Redknapp, and, in my opinion, everything changed. Gazza scored THAT goal and we won 2–0.

Immediately after the match, I noticed the stadium was still full. Even the Scotland fans weren't going anywhere. I had the assistant director of the tournament next to me and I stated, "I'm playing it." He told me that I couldn't, then he turned around and saw the Royal Box immediately behind us was empty and said, "On your head be it." I played *Three Lions* for the first time at Wembley and the entire stadium started singing along; remember this was after the match and normally people want to get home, but not today. We all sensed something special was happening; could we win our first major tournament in 30 years? It was amazing, the atmosphere was talked about on TV, even Des Lynham said that something had changed at Wembley, he wasn't sure what it was, then he commented, "It must be the music." What a high that was for me! How did I know that Des said that as I was at the match? Well, don't forget, I had a day job too. I had just been commissioned to produce all the official videos of the tournament. We weren't sure at the beginning how many releases there would be, but I had to set up an infrastructure to handle the production of up to ten releases. After every single game, I was couriered a master tape of the worldwide broadcast feed and I had a team at Banana watching as many games that were on live and logging all incidents on these basic early PCs we had – every moment, every goal, yellow card etc.

After each match at Wembley, I would drive home past our studios and start working on the video cutdowns; production was well underway. The tournament was a massive success and I felt front, middle, and centre of it all. I was introduced to Skinner and Baddiel as the DJ who, off his own back, decided to play *Three Lions* and they both thanked me. The single went to No.1, the whole country was singing it. Then came our famous 4–1 victory against Holland. There is a common misconception that that must have been the best atmosphere, but this is not true. Yes, during the game, we were in disbelief, but the game after was the quarter-final against Spain and that was by far the best pre- and post-match atmosphere. After Holland, we all believed. I told the crowd that the world was listening, the players were listening, so sing it loud and proud and boy, did they. It was spine-tingling.

I followed up on the FA's request to book the singers for the quarters, semis and final and managed to get Alison Moyet, Glenn Tilbrook, Paul Carrick and, for the semi-final, Paul Young. They were all favourites of mine and big British stars. Everything went well until England v Germany, the semi-final. I had been the DJ and announcer for many matches by now and had never put a foot wrong, but this was the biggest game in the UK for 30 years. I don't remember being especially nervous, but after the crowd sang *Three Lions*, I had to ask everyone to stand for the national anthems. Paul Young was rehearsed and in position, the Steadicam broadcasting around the globe was right in front of him and I played the opening notes of the German national anthem. I'd pressed play on the wrong CD, FUCK! I immediately pulled the fader down and those two opening notes just echoed around the stadium. Paul had already started singing, but stopped when I stopped the track. He looked up at me as if to ask, "What's going on?" but the crowd just sang. No one except poor Paul Young noticed the mistake; the opening notes of the wrong anthem sort of acting as a tuning fork for this massive pumped-up crowd, and they sang their hearts out; Paul caught up and carried on singing. There were about 76,000 people there and no one then or after ever noticed. If you look at the YouTube clip today after reading this, it's obvious, but, I've been getting away with it, all my life. Sorry, Paul, my bad.

Back at Banana, I completed production on 11 sell-through video releases. I interviewed Terry Venables at his club Scribes in Kensington for about two hours for his release and two years later was commissioned to do the same work for France 98, the World Cup. Things were going well.

Chapter 13

These are the Days

Jamie Cullum

So we were in the early to mid-nineties and life was jogging along. Banana Split Productions was growing and we had a few more staff and a few more edit suites (we ultimately grew to fourteen suites and 55 staff). The work was cool and amongst other things we were now making TV ads. I discovered that the video industry, in which I was making long-form sell-through videos, was not advertising on TV. A gap I thought, so I did my research and approached a few companies with some facts. I remember distinctly when we had babies, there was a parenting magazine that they gifted you when you left the hospital. On their back cover, there was an ad for a *Thomas The Tank Engine* video. I decided that would have cost them circa £50,000 for that ad to be placed and I looked up the cost of a two-week campaign on Channel 5's newly-launched *Milkshake* kids' TV morning shows. I decided that it would be cheaper to advertise on TV and approached Hit Entertainment with these possibly debatable facts. I made Hit's ads for a further seven or so years along with their long-form content. I had a stand-up row once with some Welsh prick young actor who was playing *Fireman Sam* with a giant latex *Fireman Sam* head on. I probably can't say that, but he was Welsh and he was a prick.

The video industry was good for me and before long I reckoned I had captured at least 80% of the UK market. TV ads included Jeremy Clarkson's first video release, *Motor Sport Mayhem*, which made its way onto *Points of View* on BBC1 for being too violent. I also put pubic hair on a Lovers Guide ad, both for Astrion. Both videos went on to sell hundreds of thousands of copies (I got away with the viewers' complaints and no one spotted the pubic hair). We started to win awards for these TV campaigns. My main client at Astrion was my friend, April; I did all her work, and then they got bought by Universal and in turn, I got all their work. April and I were a great team and went on to win many Video Home Entertainment Awards with big TV campaigns for movies like *Bridget*

Jones's Diary, where I came up with 10 x 10-second ad executions which were 10 different clips from the movie that I selected of about eight seconds each (plus the pack shot) and they played out really well.

Around this time, I made my first proper sell-through concert video starring Michael Ball. I knew Michael's dad from Wembley, as he produced the opening ceremony for Euro 96 and somehow I wangled my way in there. Michael's tour manager back then in 1993 was a man called Phil Bowdry. Phil has gone on to be one of the most important people in the world of live music and he stayed loyal to me throughout the years. I carried on shooting Michael Ball shows right up to recently with the *Ball and Boe* shows… that's over 30 years; I'm proud of that.

Once I'd produced and directed Michael, I had something to show other artists, so I put myself out there. One of my favourite stories – the bizarre encounter I mentioned earlier – is pitching for the filming of a Barry Manilow show. A video company called Telstar wanted the rights and had asked me to attend the pitch meeting with Barry's manager, Garry. I did this, and later that day, a fax went out to the four companies pitching with me copied in. He asked them all to make their best offers but stated that he wanted me to film the show. Brilliant!! He then called me to tell me he thought I was great and all I had to do was get Barry to agree and we would film the show.

I was invited down to see the tour in Bournemouth and to meet Barry after. I made all my director's notes during the show and was taken backstage to meet Barry. He said hi but wanted to get out of his stage gear, take his makeup off, and go out for dinner. Blimey! Since the time that Danielle took me to Blenheim Palace to see the *One Voice* show, I was a fan and now I was going to dinner with him… We hopped into his people carrier and there were hundreds of women on the ramp outside the venue screaming and banging their hands onto the van. Barry humbly told me that he couldn't believe he still got this reaction and seemed truly blown away. We had a pizza in the basement of a local hotel and I told him how I wanted to shoot the show and an idea I had for a TV special. I dropped names of favourite songs so he knew I knew his music, and it seemed to go really well. We were staying in the same hotel, and after we went to our respective rooms, a knock came on my door; it was Mark, Barry's assistant, who was with us that night and he told me I'd done great and Barry wanted to see the Michael Ball show I had just made. I got up early, went to HMV in town and bought a copy of my own video. All I had to do was get him to like me and I was there. We got on great. I remember calling my editor, Rory, who was also a fan and telling him we got it.

After the weekend, I went into the office as normal on Monday morning and a tannoy call came over the telephone system to the whole office (I wasn't by my desk) saying that Barry Manilow was on the phone for me. I didn't believe it was him. I thought it was a friend who I might have told my exciting news to over the weekend. "Hello Barry," I answered chirpily and somewhat sarcastically. "Hi Steve," came back Barry's voice. Fuck, it was him. He went on to tell me he thought I was great but something had spooked him on the previous night's show in Brighton (apparently, the stage got 'rushed' by some over-enthusiastic fans and maybe a couple were hurt), but he wasn't in the right headspace to have the show filmed; he was keen that I understood that it wasn't me, it was him. Fuck! Gone as quickly as I thought I had it, I was gutted.

Two weeks later, the tour arrived at Wembley Arena and I got a call from Mark saying Barry wanted to see me after the London show that night. I'm back on,

I thought. I took my friend Monique along, made more notes, they gave us fourth row seats, and I went backstage to see Barry; brilliant, I'm going to get the gig after all that.

Barry took me to the side, looked into my eyes, told me how talented I was and said that he really wanted me to understand that it wasn't me, it was him. Oh Jesus, really? I laughed and said I understood, "We'll do another tour." "We will,' he replied, and off I fucked. As I am writing these memoirs, I am currently in negotiations with Garry for Barry's last-ever show in London at The Palladium. We've had four long phone calls and plenty of emails. I've recced The Palladium, met the promotor, and whilst typing, he isn't answering any of my recent emails; it's been three weeks. Maybe I'll be able to confirm that Barry and I just aren't meant to be by the end of this book. I just heard… he's not doing it… again!

I also made pop videos in those days; the budgets weren't great but they were creative and fun. I made one with the fabulous Craig David at our studios and his guest stars were a very young Rita Ora and Tinchy Strider, what star Rita became. The Ministry of Sound hired me to make a video for a dance tune by a singer called Michelle Weeks. I'd never been to Las

Vegas so I came up with an idea to shoot there, along the strip and in the desert, it was great. The only trouble was the budget and after 48 hours there, with jet lag, I had to come home. I'd only ever flown economy in those days; I simply couldn't afford anything else. It was on this flight home that I promised myself that I would never fly economy transatlantic again, ever. To this day, I have not.

When Ministry promoted the single in the UK, they had an appearance on *Blue Peter* and the product manager, a young girl called Claire, asked me to find them some dancers for the appearance. Easy, I knew dancers; I could book them and get them rehearsed and help out. I charged Claire £500 per dancer and paid them £300. After they did the job, I got an essay of a fax from Claire. It seems she asked the dancers what they were being paid and discovered the fact that I was making a margin. To this day, I believe it's important in business/life that everyone understands and respects that we all deserve to make a living. Claire didn't seem to follow that concept. In her essay fax, she said that it had only taken me "5 minutes" to book those dancers. I crossed out "5 minutes", replaced it with "15 years", and sent the fax back.

Chapter 14

Let's Get Physical

Olivia Newton-John

One day in 1999, I was called into VCI's offices to meet a senior executive called Richard Percy. VCI was the largest independent video distribution company in the UK at the time, I had perhaps started to make a couple of ads for them at that point. Prior to the meet, Richard had told me he wanted me to make a fitness video for him and I decided that this was a new and exciting market that I really wanted to get into. I hadn't made one before, but I had a feeling that they were going to get big.

Before arriving, I decided I could do it for £15k. I wanted in and I thought if I do the first one very cost effectively, I could get my foot in the door. I sat down at Richard's desk and he explained how he had an output deal with Yorkshire Television and needed my help. He wanted me to make this fitness video with an actress called Glenda McKay, who was a star on *Emerdale*, but he only had a £60k budget. My face didn't flicker. I explained that it wouldn't be easy at that price but I would make it work as I wanted to get in with VCI and that it was more about 'jam tomorrow' for me. Brilliant! I got five times what I was looking for and made a great video at Yorkshire TV studios in Leeds with Glenda and her gang, who were all lovely.

There is a story about that production and a lot of paint, but I can't be arsed to write it; call me if you really want to know it. I went on in my career to make over 180 fitness videos, and as far as I'm concerned, that genre put my kids through private school. I worked with some great artists during this time and three of the worst ever. See if you can guess from this list who were the absolute worst: Kate Lawler, Nell McAndrew, Geri Halliwell, Martine McCutcheon, assorted *Big Brother* stars including Jade Goody (who for the record was fabulous and really hard working), Jordon (the model) and Nadia a transgender winner of *Big Brother*, Liberty X, and Denise Welsh, who fell pregnant with her now superstar son, Matty Healy from The 1975, during production. Denise's video was shot near Marbella in

Spain and her husband, Tim Healy, and I enjoyed a cheeky smoke on my balcony after the shoot; he was a solid bloke who I liked a lot. What I will also never forget is Denise's agent, a lady called Lindsay Granger. One day, Lindsay and I had to go to Manchester on the train to get Denise to sign the deal and do a photo shoot. Denise was playing the landlady of the Rovers Return in *Coronation Street* and we did the photo shoot at Granada TV, nothing special there… on the way back much later in the day, Lindsay and I had a long journey home to London and naturally we chatted. She spoke about her father, who was an actor. Hold on, I thought, Lindsay had a deep, resonant voice for a lady and a rich American accent. "Are you related to Stuart Granger?" I enquired. "He's my dad," she replied. Well, the stories of Hollywood greats flowed. What a great train ride that was.

Back to who the baddies were, well, for this version of the book, I'm going to tell you. Nadia from *Big Brother* and Martine were crazy and really difficult to work with. Martine's video ended up being quite beautiful but I remember leaving that set to go back on holiday and not saying goodbye, something I would never normally do. A few months later, she called me from the set of a TV talent show that she was judging on to tell me she was with my friends Michael Ball and Billy Sammeth, her fellow judges on this ITV prime time show; Billy was a fabulous friend who famously managed Cher, KC and the Sunshine Band and the glorious Joan Rivers. The phone call with Martine was friendly as if nothing untoward had happened, I hear she is a lot more chilled and lovely these days.

These fitness videos went on and on for years and the budgets went as high as £300k. My fantasy woman back then might have been Sharon Stone so I asked her agent if she fancied making one of these videos. The lady agent, who's name I can't recall, invited me plus one to Wimbledon to discuss the idea as she also looked after Serena Williams. I took my friend Simon as he was a big tennis fan and we met in the players lounge and then were given tickets to centre court to sit in the family box to see Serena and others play. Sharon declined my kind offer but Simon and I had a Wimbledon experience neither of us will forget.

The two best stories for this chapter on fitness videos are Geri Halliwell and the Ministry of Sound. They both happened a bit later in my life but I think I should club them together here. Geri was a HUGE star. She'd recently left the Spice Girls and she was papped doing Yoga at George Michael's villa in Saint Tropez. The pictures were on every tabloid's front page. I sent a well-constructed facsimile to Andy Stephens, who was Geri's manager (and George Michael's). As I stood by the fax machine, no sooner had it gone through, the reply immediately came back with a hand-written "No thanks!". I had offered £250k which I hadn't even got backed up by a deal with any of the video distributors. I didn't have the money but was confident I could get it. I immediately crossed out the £250,000 and made it £500,000. Andy called me straight back and a few days later, we did the deal with my friend Paul at VCI. At the time, my biggest competitor was Brian Klein who ran OTB Productions; I didn't know Brian so well back then but he did most of VCI's long-form work (except fitness) and that pissed me off. Years later, Brian is now one of my best industry friends and he told me that he had been asked by Paul to sign Geri Halliwell, but he couldn't get management over the line. So he had to call Paul to say it was impossible and Paul had to tell him that I had bought the deal in. We had a good laugh in 2024 when he recounted this to me; I had no idea. Here I was (getting away with it), offering money I didn't have before even having the backing of a distributor. This became my model thereafter; I had a sense of what things were worth and just went ahead as if I had the money. This process never let me down, ever. Well I say that, I did once offer Atomic Kitten £50,000 for a sell-through and I could't get the money. I made the videos (two of them) anyhow and Martin, their manager, is still my great friend today, although he still thinks I owe him £50 grand.

I'll never forget the Geri shoots; the first was on 9/11, a day that none of us will ever forget, We heard about the planes going into the Twin Towers in New York, when we were on a break and watching the TV in the green room, we all thought that the planes were small light aircraft and carried on filming. By lunchtime, the terrible facts were emerging and I thought I would try and keep the news from Geri. No such luck, at lunch time in her dressing room she was on her mobile phone. We did carry on filming but it all felt very surreal. The second video was in Malibu near Los Angeles, which was a wonderful place to shoot and where I had to pay Geri's favourite make-up artist £5,000 a day, easily the equivalent of £15,000 a day today – mental times. I just couldn't imagine how we should or could pay a make-up artist that much money for two days' work, but Geri was the star and we made it work. I can't remember his name, but I have to report that he was an absolute delight and kept Geri chilled all day long.

Another fitness job worth mentioning was one for Penny Lancaster; she was Rod Stewart's girlfriend at the time and was lovely. I went to Rod's home in Essex and we ended up shooting it in Rod's 'back yard' in Palm Beach, Florida, where he had his own private beach. When I recced the house, there was only a maid there to show me around. I asked to look in the room "up there" as it looked like a great shot. It turned out to be Rod's palatial master bedroom. He was great; he even went out in his Ferrari to get us coffees. At the end of the shoot, I was waiting in his kitchen for Penny to sign her release form, and the phone on the kitchen table where I was sitting started to ring. It rang for ages and ages; after about two minutes of incessant ringing, I heard Rod pick it up in the utility room. "HELLO," he screamed just as the other end had obviously put the phone down. "Well, fuck off then," he yelled as he slammed the phone down, gave me a wink, and strolled off with the ghetto blaster he'd asked me for earlier. I had told him it wasn't mine to give, but he said he wanted it for his kids and just took it after we'd wrapped. It was fair, as he didn't charge us for the location. Rod was funny and lovely and fully supportive of the lady who would become his wife and she was super lovely too.

Towards the end of Banana, someone from a record

company called me to say they thought I should try and do a fitness video with the girls (and one guy) from the No. 1 smash hit video, *Call On Me by Eric Prydz*. I thought this was a great idea and immediately went around the industry to see if anyone wanted it. No one did; it was October and all their release schedules were set. I told the Ministry and they asked if I wanted to do it with them; they would do the marketing and distribution and I would produce at cost; we would be 50/50 partners. I immediately said yes, as I thought it would be a big hit. Deep into pre-production, Lohan, the boss at Ministry, called me to ask if I realised I would be responsible for half the losses if it didn't work. Naively I didn't realise this at all and agreed to a reduced profit split – a 70/30 deal in their favour. When the video was released, it was HUGE, it went to No. 1 and I earned the most out of any one project I had ever earned. It was also my last year of an earn-out and would therefore be worth a lot more on a multiple to me, but I'm not at that stage of my story yet, so hang on.

Walking Heads

Dad

King Eric at one of those United gigs

Baby Driver in Brooklyn

Mum's 80th

Shirlie and Pepsi at the Video Café

That one and only ever photo card

The very nice Russell Watson
and the professor

Saskia looking sleepy

Dad and the three of us in Spain 1982

Me and Sash in Beverly Hills

Holocaust surviving legend
Ziggy shipper

My kids

Harry Kane doing a toy ad at Sassy

Best course ever? Royal County Down

Fitness video shoot with Glenda McKay

Video Café with Anthony

Me and PK

My mate Tony Gibber

This is the jacket Spalter used to steal

Me and Posner working at Disney Land in the early 90s for our Prince

An early JC ad

The wonderful Barbara Windsor
when we shot a lotto ad

Lila & me in Amsterdam

Drysie, PK and me at my sedate stag

That first ever multi-cam shoot with Michael Jackson - Cannes mid 90s

Central London Radio

An early DJ gig

Papa Issi, The nicest man I ever knew

Mum & us three and that perm

Two Stevie's

Two DJ's - GC & me

Wedding time

Me, PK and our mum

On England duty around the country by helicopter

Directing a Nick Heyward pop video

That's a big camera

It's nice when we all get together

My boys and me

Provence selfie

Mum

Chapter 15

Work Hard

Depeche Mode

I'm gonna dump a bunch of formative work stories here, these were exciting years for me and I got to meet and enjoy working with a huge variety of folk, often with a story to boot.

The legendary Billy Sammeth and I became great friends when I did a deal to co-produce and direct *Joan Rivers Live at The London Palladium*. Joan was to be my partner; she was amazing but also a bit crazy. On the night of the show, she told me to get rid of all the cameras as she was too nervous to shoot this particular show. She came onto the stage at the Palladium with all her giant handwritten notes prepared and wanted to plaster them to the front of the stage. She was a bit manic, so I just said it would be ok and I would change a couple of shots… There were two hours to go before curtain. Billy, my affable friend, sorted it.

Joan came into Banana Split to edit the video with me. Now, she was a true star; she knew what she wanted, she was demanding but I had every respect for her immense talent. It was ok that she was a bit highly strung; she had earned the right. She made a great partner on the production, and the DVD and TV airing did really well. A few years later, I booked Joan for a massive gig in the Maldives, but more about that later.

I started to make more and more comedy videos for the likes of *Little Britain*, which was a huge show that we filmed in Blackpool. Matt and David are wonderful artists, super clever and very hard-working. That show was a challenging one for them to do and the tour was long and hard, but it's a testament to an age before political correctness, and I'm proud to have produced it. I shot Dave Spikey, Tim Vine and many others. I'm just about to direct Tim's new show this year in 2024. Comedy is bloody easy work; it's shrouded in mystery, only to be known by those who have done it before; they are the trusted experts, including my friend Brian Klein who has done some massive gigs but as he would admit, you just get the right crew, light it well and point your cameras at the talent; easy peasy. Well, it is for us because we know what we are doing….

Concert sell-through videos were also big for me; I produced and directed loads, including David Cassidy, the previously-mentioned Michael Ball several times, John Barrowman multiple times and Donny Osmond (who was a delight) and wanted to remix the sound himself. We swapped phone numbers and one day, he called my home just as Belinda was bathing the kids, and asked to speak to me. "Who's calling?" my wife asked sharply. "It's Donny," came the response. Now, Belinda was a huge Donny Osmond fan in the seventies, his posters were all over her bedroom wall. She thought it was someone dicking around and just said that I was at the office and to call me there, promptly putting the phone down. Later that night, I explained that it really was Donny. "NO!!" she screamed, then "NO!" again, with her hands over her face… it was funny, perhaps slightly more so for me than Belinda, who was mortified. I went to see Donny in Ireland prior to filming in London.

His stage outfit was a very old fashioned woollen roll-neck jumper, so I promised him a selection of shirts to try when he got to London; it would be my gift. I arranged for Harvey Nichols to bring over a rack and we chose a really cool Dolce & Gabbana one; little did I know when telling Donny it looked great that it was £890! Donny was so receptive to my director's notes and welcomed any feedback after the Irish show. I told him he had to sing *Puppy Love* the way the fans remembered it as he was messing with it a bit; he got it. I also told him that he was too much of a legend to encourage them to clap along. There was a really obvious moment when he was on top of the steps of the stage design during his hit *Soldier of Love*; I told him he only needed to put his arm in the air and they would do it. When it came to the London show, he did just that and it worked like a dream – the shots were amazing. Several years later, I filmed Donny again in Las Vegas and he was as gorgeous as ever.

The concert work continued to build nicely. There are several dressing room stories, like the time Russell Watson wanted me to check if his make-up was too orange about six minutes before he was due on stage with a 76-piece orchestra already in place. I said he was fine, but he fired the make-up artist anyway and re-did it himself. Russell doesn't have the best reputation in the business, but I thought he was lovely, polite, and respectful. I visited his home studio up north somewhere and he made me a cuppa, so he can't be all bad.

John Barrowman called me into his dressing room at The Albert Hall once to discuss how I was going to shoot the show (in an hour's time). I listened. He looked up, clocked the expression on my face and said, "Fuck it, you know what you're doing."… by then, I did.

I'm sad to report that David Cassidy was a bitter man; nice to me, but bitter about how much fame he had to endure and how little money he had later in life… I shot many, many more shows at all the great London venues, Wembley, The Royal Albert Hall, and the great Hammersmith Odeon, where my obsession for concerts began. Sell-through videos on both VHS and later DVD were seen as the poor relation to television, but not by me. Ever. In fact, I always did and always thought the opposite was true, and my career path seems to have proved this to be the case.

I once made a documentary called *The Story of London's Underworld* and met some proper scary people, none more so than one notorious villain called Joey Pile. I was interviewing him in a pub garden in deepest, darkest South London, and he told me he had gone to prison for murder in the sixties but that it wasn't him; it was a stray bullet. Quick as a flash, I asked him if there were a lot of stray bullets around in those days. He stared at me for a good few seconds, I felt my stomach churn, and then he laughed and said, "I suppose there were."

Dave Courtney, the celebrity tough nut, was an interesting character. When I finished my second video with him, he told me if I EVER needed a favour to call him. I never did. Blimey, the things you do to put your kids through private school.

I produced and directed virtually the entire output of our company in those days. Other docs included a collaboration with The Sunday Times called *100 Stories of the Sporting Century* and *Wembley: Venue of Legends*, which I thought I was uniquely qualified to do.

I distinctly remember filming of *The Nativity* at The Young Vic, starring Toby Jones. Nothing super special so far, but it was presented in the round, and when it came to post-production, the edit was a real challenge, one of the most challenging I've ever undertaken in my career to date. We did a good job along with a great editor I had back then called Chris

Hall and the video was a minor hit. Not easy, but so satisfying back then to meet the challenge head-on.

I would rarely take on corporate video work as it was dull. However, in the mid-nineties and through my work at Wembley Stadium I managed to wrangle Coca Cola as a client. I met their Head of Marketing at a Coca Cola Cup final and I sent her my showreel with a note which included the words: "I know the chances of you reading this letter are slim and watching the showreel even slimmer but I'm giving it a go." She did read the letter and view the tape and I went on to produce videos for them for several years thereafter.

The only production that still makes me feel a little queasy was the filming of a brand new giant sign going up at the iconic Piccadilly Circus. It was supposed to be lifted into place by a giant hydraulic lift at just after midnight. My crew and I waited for two hours and nothing… I went home and told them to wait until 4am and if nothing appeared to go home, which is what they did. Imagine my horror when the client called on Monday morning to ask how the filming went, only to be told that the truck shut down Piccadilly Circus at 5am. I felt sick to my stomach, we missed it. It was their fault as the instructions in writing were simply wrong and we waited an extra four hours. The sign was never going up again and I think the client and I conspired to never let her bosses know about this monumental fuck up. And that wasn't the only time that things had gone wrong.

I made a film for Top Shop starring Gok Wan who was very nice and very professional. The filming itself took place on a Saturday and was unremarkable. What was remarkable was what we call the 'de-rig and get out'. I had the kit and crew all in my Range Rover as there was only room for my car in the very old-fashioned car lift at the Arcadia HQ (Top Shop's parent company). We de-rigged quickly and all wanted to get home to our respective Saturday nights. I remember I had a dinner party to go to. I drove my big car into this 'car lift' and it was a very tight squeeze, the lift doors closed behind us. I had four passengers, all crew, as I let Gok leave straight after filming. The idea in those car lifts is that when you are in you wind down the windows for air and to press the relevant buttons to take you back up to street level. The problem was the lift didn't respond to my button pressing. We were locked in there without the ability to open our car doors and the fucking lift was going nowhere. So I did what I had to do which was press the emergency alarm button, nothing. One of us had one bar of reception on our mobile phone and managed to call 999. Five hours later, the fire brigade got the lift to work after cutting their way through the roof of this 1960s car lift, sparks flying everywhere and somehow getting the mechanism working again. Many farts later all five of us drove out into the London summer air and breathed a huge collective sigh of relief, got home and all missed our respective plans for that Saturday night.

Gok is a very talented presenter and I cannot fully explain to you how different presenting to camera is to being a confident public speaker or even an actor. Those who present are experts, they are naturals who have spent years crafting their art. Barry Davis, the legendary sports commentator, Cat Deely, Ben Shepherd, Tess Daley, Vernon Kaye, Alex Zane and many more who I have worked with over the years are so gifted at what they do, it's effortless. Make a golf video in Spain with a very talented celebrity golf instructor and the instruction bits, the body of the work, are faultless. Ask him to walk over a small bridge and say, "Hello, my name is Gareth Benson." – fucking hysterical… Maybe 20 takes?

One time, a very successful entrepreneur called Julian Richer hired me to produce and direct a series of high-end corporate training videos that he wanted to sell for an exorbitant price. I had lunch with the very charismatic Mr Richer and he bought along his friend, Ray Kelvin, who was "Ted Baker" in real life. Julian was Business Communicator of the Year and insisted he wanted to just sit down at his desk and talk to the camera. I very strongly suggested this wasn't a good idea and he should write the scripts with a scriptwriter and have the whole thing on auto-cue. That I insisted would make the filming a lot easier. He told me I was being a baby and he would be fine. On the first day of filming, he couldn't get his words out. The cameras and hot lights unnerved him and his tongue kept sticking to the roof of his mouth. I was trying not to smile whilst at my director's bridge of monitors when after about an hour of fluffs he growled, "Kemsley, you cunt – you were right." He was pissed off. We got it done in the end but it took a lot longer.

The music work was my passion and I once delayed going on holiday as Michael Bublé's record company hired me to make four films with Michael for his first album. He was so, so nice and the work was great. He told his manager that I was a really cool director – that made my month! I did a few films with Lisa Stansfield, some pop promos, and I remember shooting her live at Ronnie Scotts. The venue was (and still is) so small I had to shoot the show twice as I could only fit three cameras in there. I shot the band in the afternoon to afford me three cameras on Lisa that night. We then edited it all together and no one was any the wiser... that's being a producer, right there.

Sometimes I get closer with the talent and after working with presenter Gloria Hunniford, actor Andrew Sachs and legendary darts commentator Sid Waddell, each was fascinated with the Jewish tradition of Friday night dinner, so I invited them all together one Friday night. Sid was hysterical, so quick-witted. Gloria and her husband Stephen were lovely and having Manuel from *Fawlty Towers* in our house was very special indeed. It was a wonderful period; my work was making me money and affording me the best of times.

One other genre that I absolutely loved was working in theatre. My friend Nicholas Lazarus introduced me to Adam Kenwright who was the nephew of legendary producer Bill Kenwright and a theatre supremo himself. Adam had his own theatre promotions company called AKA and they asked me to work on some incredible theatre productions. We became their de-facto production company and I loved the work so much that I did all of it personally. There is something very special about working in a theatre; I learnt quickly there are rules and traditions that one must abide by but the talent I got to shoot with were amazing. Plays like *Birdsong* where I was allowed to direct with Sir Trevor Nunn sitting right by me as he was directing the play that starred Gillian Anderson. We created EPKs (electronic press kits) with lots of clips of the production that I shot. *Rock of Ages* was bloody great and I was re-acquainted with one of its producers Tony Smith who managed Genesis and Phil Collins. I was thrilled to work alongside Jerry Mitchell and Sonia Freedman on *Legally Blonde*, which starred one of the best actors of her generation, Sheridan Smith. Jerry was so kind and encouraging, Sheridan was sublime and Sonia was… a bit terse. Sonia is a big-time theatre producer with lots of hits under her belt and, somewhat archetypal, she walks around with her little pet dog everywhere. I made a pop video to promote the show with Sheridan, Duncan James from Blue and the cast at Elstree Studios. Jerry had approved the concept and we were going for a Busby Berkeley over-head shot. It's a famous shot first developed in the great musicals of the '50s which was directly over the top of the cast who were fanning out in a synchronised style. I had agreed with Jerry to build a stage to get

166

some height to make the shot work (Jerry left all the video directing to me), but the shot wasn't working so I made the decision to break down the staging which had cost a pretty penny and do it all on the studio floor. After lunch, Sonia arrived with her little dog and I greeted her at the studio doors. "Who made the decision to lose the stage?" she snapped. "Me," I responded. "Wrong decision," she fired back and walked off. I felt sick, she was my client and wasn't happy. I didn't show any of my fear and just carried on. When I sent her the final cut she sent me an email that said the promo was "truly inspirational work". Maybe that was her style and the way she gets the best out of people. I found her distant and not so friendly.

We worked on so many West End shows back then; I made a really fun promo video with Amanda Holden, Richard Blackwood, Nigel Lindsay and Nigel Harman for *Shrek The Musical* at Air Studios to the track "I'm a believer". Working with talented stars is pure joy and directing them is easy. We shot an ad for that show in 3D which meant my long-suffering Director of Photography, Phil Bradshaw, had to schlepp around London with TWO very heavy cameras on a Steadicam rig until the early hours. You needed two cameras to shoot 3D and they were heavy cameras as it was being shot for cinemas. AKA then decided after maybe three years of this fun work to start their own in-house video department, which I got in principle but I knew it wouldn't produce work as good as we were doing and sure enough we were called back within a couple of years to work on new productions like *9 to 5* with the very funny Brian Conley and Louise Redknapp who was a bit grumpy with me at first (I think she thought I was someone else) but super chill in the end. I've mentioned before that I never liked shooting to storyboards as I found the process too restrictive. What I would do instead is shoot the film using my team and a handy cam (latterly my phone), we wouldn't light anything but we'd sketch out the film with rough shots that I would shoot myself and then I'd edit a test film to play with before the actual shoot date. It made the whole process a little more efficient on the main filming day when top talent had less time for faffing around waiting for me to work out what I wanted.

My attitude to directing was simple, I knew I could visualise the shots I wanted and I knew I had the ability to explain that vision to those I worked with, whether cameramen, exec producers, DOP's or the talent (actors). How did I know what was going to work and what wouldn't? I don't know I just knew, it was in me and I was very confident that my way was the right way. I hindsight I'm glad I never had partners or bosses who were directors as well, as there would have been creative differences. I was rarely ever challenged, if I was hired as the director, I was the boss and it was my responsibility to deliver a film that worked. It always did and my confidence grew year on year. Today I am sure I can handle any shoot anywhere in the world hence my ambition to make 'that movie'. Directing is easy when you surround yourself with great talent, all you have to do is lead and take responsibility which I love to do.

Chapter 16

And the beat goes on
The Whispers

As I think back to this time, I do believe that my skill sets were not just creative, as entrepreneurship played a big part in what we were achieving. What is entrepreneurship? I think it's the ability to take calculated risks but also being able to hire good people and nurture them. It's the same skill set as being a good dad I thought and judging by the letters and messages from staff I have received over the years, I did ok. I thought I was a kind and encouraging boss, but one day at Banana, I swept past a young editor called Andy (he went on to marry a cousin of mine). As we passed on the stairs, he stiffened and went flat back against the wall. "What are you doing?" I asked cheerily. "Have you any idea how scary you are?" he replied... I really didn't. I knew I had a loud and deep voice, which I used to good effect throughout my life, but I didn't think I was scary. I decided it wasn't a bad thing and would balance my kindness… at least that's what I thought, and with a career where my average member of staff stayed with me well over 12 years, I still think I was right. During a long career, I believe I have hired well over 200 people, but I've only fired a handful. Sometimes that's easy because they've lied, stolen or been a complete idiot. In my time, I've had all three of those. Mostly, I have had folk "move on" after at least five or six years and those meetings have been emotional. I always kept a box of tissues in my office for emotional staff one-on-ones. My team was an extension of my family and I cared for them all dearly whilst they were with me. An amazing fact is that I've had four children via staff, well, not really, but there are three couples all who met and stayed at work whilst they began dating, two are married with kids, and one couple is still very much together with the male, who I shouldn't name – Adam – seemingly refusing to get married… we have ribbed him about this in many a Secret Santa.

During my career, I have undertaken hundreds and hundreds of interviews; I see the interview process as crucial. Having a great team around you is probably the number one most important element behind any entrepreneur's success. However, when I interviewed potential staff, I rarely got to the five-minute mark before I had made my mind up about them. I often had to stretch out interviews to 15 minutes just to be respectful. Many times, I offered people jobs on the spot, asking what they were earning now and either offering them more, or less but with more promise. I always wanted to find out about their family backgrounds. I wasn't looking for privilege, just a work ethic. If their parents were teachers or nurses, I felt more affinity with a hard worker than sometimes to those from a more privileged background.

All my staff have a story about their interview. I often left them spinning and unsure if I was serious. So I came up with a strategy of asking another member of the team to give them a tour of the studios; without fail, they would ask, "He just offered me the job; was he serious?" "Oh, yes," always came the response.

I mentioned earlier that I wrote to 83 record companies for a junior position when I was 17 and didn't get one interview, let alone a job. I was determined to see as many people as I could when I was a boss, if only to offer advice. Lots of friends and acquaintances asked me to see their kids or friend's kids if they wanted a job "in media"; I always said yes. One of the first questions I would ask was what part of media they were interested in and so many simply didn't know. We had at least six career paths in our small business and there were so many more out there. I always encourage young people to try and figure out what their ambitions are. You don't have to have ambitions but it does help if you go for an interview that you have a small clue as to what your future might be in an ideal world. To the teenager who came in to see me and answered my question – "Why are we here today then?" – with "I dunno, my mum sent me", and to the one who said his real ambition was to be a pilot, sorry that your interviews only lasted 30 seconds and I hope you are both doing well today.

Overall my attitude to my business's was essentially to do great work, deliver on time to the agreed budget and then the money would take care of it's self. Clearly this is simplistic and you do have to keep a constant eye on the detail, but if you are cut out for leadership your gut will tell you most of what you need to know. Trust your instincts they are almost always right and if not… you'll figure it out.

Back at home, our boys were growing older and it was soon to be off-to-school time. We looked at three schools in Mill Hill and there was one that I saw on my own called Grimsdell. It was by far the most expensive and by far the best. I called Belinda and said that Joe had to go there, it was amazing. She said that she thought we couldn't afford it and she was right, we couldn't, but we sent him there anyway and Louis the year after. It was the start of an amazing education in the Mill Hill School Foundation for all three of our kids and somehow each term I came up with the money. Typing this today and recalling this time, it was madness, reckless, but I had been getting away with it (all my life) up to this point, and I thought that with hard work and luck, this would continue, and it did, well, almost. Home life was good. We did discuss having another child, maybe we might get a girl, but we were happy with our boys, and our attitude about a third was relaxed.

Then, one day, Belinda discovered she was pregnant, which we were both happy about; maybe I was a bit nervous about the associated costs, but this child would be four years away from any form of private education, which by now was 'de rigour'. On a Saturday lunch time, I was on my way to watch Spurs play United and Belinda called me crying and asked me to come home immediately. Without getting into too much detail, it was absolutely obvious she had miscarried. She was terribly upset, so we called the gynaecologist, Richard, and the next morning, we went to Watford General for the procedure. Richard scanned Belinda and said that he didn't know what that was yesterday but there's still a heartbeat there and that we should go home. We were shell-shocked but after some time, we both decided that Saskia Eve Kemsley, the baby girl that arrived in June 1999, had a twin that didn't survive. I still feel sure of that today. When Saskia was born, I don't think I have ever (to this day) sobbed as much as I did. She came out purple and didn't make a sound for ages. She then spent her first week in an incubator, which was scary, but all's well that ends well and our family was complete with this baby daughter, our miracle child. Having only had boys prior, I remember nappy changing was a whole different experience. Sassy, as we soon called her, was gorgeous; she was and still is our princess. In those early years, she spent time dressing up as one, although her hair wouldn't grow, she was still very beautiful and we all adored her. It did of course grow in the end.

Family is very important to me, Belinda's late father's parents perished in the Holocaust and her dad was put on the famous Kinder Transport from Austria to England. He was five years old and was split from his brother. Arriving with no money, and speaking no English, he went on to qualify as an architect and become a successful builder. One day, when I was in an edit suite at Banana Split, I got a phone call from someone purporting to represent Warner Brothers Wow, I thought, I'd love them as a client. The young man, it turned out, didn't really work for Warners, he was just selling ad space in a brochure for the premiere of a full-length documentary movie called *Into The Arms of Strangers*, all to benefit The Princes Trust. I had no idea what the movie was about but said that I would take out the ad if the Head of Marketing at Warners would watch our showreel. In fairness to the lad, he made it happen and I got a meeting with the Head of Marketing. Brilliant, I thought. Not really, as it turned out that her boyfriend ran one of my competitors and I didn't stand a chance of getting their business at that point in time.

A few weeks later, as a paid-up advertiser, I received two tickets to the Royal Premiere of this film and I wasn't really bothered about going until, one night, I got home late and found Belinda already reading in bed. I recognised the cover artwork for the book she was reading as the same as the tickets I had just received. I asked her what the book was about and she told me it was about the Kinder Transport which is how her father arrived in the UK to escape the Nazis. Wow, that was weird. I told her I had tickets to see a Royal Premiere movie release of the same title; it must been the same story as the artwork was the same. We went to the premiere in a tiny cinema in Leicester Square. Prince Charles attended and we both watched the feature-length doc in a state of emotional amazement. One of the main architects of the Kinder Transport was Nicholas Winton (you have to see the *That's Life* clip on YouTube to really get it). He was sitting directly in front of us. I was awestruck. If this man didn't do what he did, I wouldn't have the three children I have. Belinda's father would never had made it over to the UK and would have almost certainly perished as an Austrian Jew in the Holocaust. It was the most surreal evening. Prince Charles was a few feet away, everyone was crying at the story, but there was added weight for us. It was almost too much to take in.

I talked earlier about Belinda's promise at the Wailing Wall that if we were to have a child and it was a boy we would come back and Barmitzvah him at the Kotel (the holiest site in Judaism) in Jerusalem. Well, we did, and this is where something else amazing happened. The Barmitzvah and the lunch after were among the most special moments of all of our lives.

We only invited immediate family and our friend, Suzi, organised the whole thing; it was spiritual and truly magical. The day after, the whole family, 26 of us, went to Yad Vashem, which is the Holocaust museum just outside Jerusalem. We split into smaller groups, and my sons, Dad, brother, nephews, and the rabbi started the tour of this emotionally shattering memorial museum. Whilst walking around, Michol, the rabbi, exclaimed, "Look! Joe." He was pointing at a sealed perspex unit with a Sefer Torah enclosed. It seemed the Torah was rescued from beneath some floorboards in Amsterdam during the war to save the holy scriptures from being burnt. The scroll seemed to be opened on the same portion that Joe had read at the Wall yesterday. The rabbi was blown away as he read it to double-check and confirmed that this completely sealed box had a Torah opened on the same piece that was Joe's Barmitzvah portion – one of hundreds of paragraphs that make up this holy scripture. We were all flabbergasted. As we finished our tour in silence, I met up with Belinda and her younger brother, David, who had been to the microfiche centre to dig out a copy of their late father's testimony. All survivors who visited Yad Vashem testified as to who their parents and grandparents were and where they believe they perished in the camps. Belinda showed me the printout of Frank's signed testimony. It was signed in 1976 on the exact same day as we were there 18 years later. The very same day. It was all very emotional, spiritual and ultimately up lifting. This series of coincidences were in my view the universe providing us with these glorious moments, or maybe it was God… who knows?

Chapter 17

Stadium Arcadium

Red Hot Chilli Peppers

The nineties continued and were good to us all. Wembley was cool and I even started to get asked to DJ the winners of the Cup Final team's parties. I did Everton once and my team Man Utd three times. The United parties were amazing; it was the first team squad only with a plus one, so it was all very private. That dodgy head of security, Ned Kelly (look him up), was on the door and it felt like we were the only outsiders in there. The pictures I still have are amazing as were the parties. Players like Cantona, Mark Hughes, Brian Robson, Lee Sharpe, Ryan Giggs, Schmeichel, Paul Ince, Bruce and Pallister were all there. These were great winning years for United, great parties and probably the greatest United team.

Around about this time, I got asked to DJ at various other stadiums, sometimes just to teach their DJs how I did my thing at Wembley, and then, one time, I got a phone call from the home of England rugby, Twickenham. The team there had become aware of what I was doing at Wembley and wanted something similar for England rugby. They asked me if I would give it a go, so I said yes. I negotiated the same fee that I got for Wembley, which was £500; although I wasn't the biggest rugby fan, this was a prestigious gig and the extra money was always useful. My first match was to be England v USA. When I arrived, I was shown up to the large tower at the stadium where there was a small team of statisticians and the like and I believe the group included the previous announcer. At the time, I ignored my suspicions that this group were VERY old school, and they and I wouldn't mix well. I just kept calm and did my thing. The tannoy mic was a stupid little supermarket microphone and I was so high up that I couldn't really feel or read the action as I felt I needed to. I had a TV and I had these 'chaps' with their red wine, sandwiches and cravats. It all felt quite unprofessional to me. England won the game by nearly 90 points and at a certain point during the second half, Ben Cohen scored a try for England. As he was running down the line, one of these cravat fucks yelled out, "Go on, Moisha." I sharply retorted, "What did you say? Did you just call him Moisha, because you think he's Jewish?" "Steady on, old boy, meant nothing by it," he replied. "Firstly," I snapped, "he's not Jewish, but I fucking am." I calmly announced the try, saw out the rest of the game with deafening silence from the cravat fucks and left for what I thought would be the last time.

As soon as I got in the car, the marketing department called to see how I felt about the gig. I told them what had happened and that I wouldn't be coming back. They said that was the exact type of thing they were trying to get rid of at the RFU. I told them the whole experience was crap, being up there, not being in control of all the music, the microphone, everything. They said they were sorry and, if I didn't mind, they would call me back during the week, but I felt I was done with them. They did call back that Wednesday. They had fired the 'cravat fucks', told me they were building me a platform at the end of the players' tunnel, on the halfway line at pitch level, setting up a TV, CD players and wanted to give me full control. I said yes and stayed for five years, seeing some of the greatest rugby matches England have ever played at that famous stadium. England v South Africa in 2002 was particularly memorable – I don't think I've ever had to substitute more players and seen more blood! What a game! 32–31 in England's favour; it was epic and *Swing Low* was sung with so much gusto as was *Jerusalem*. Rugby League also asked me to do the big international test matches between Great Britain and Australia at Wembley, Hull and Old Trafford. To this day, the second test at Old Trafford in 1997 was the best atmosphere I have ever heard in a stadium. I was in the centre of the pitch to announce the team walkouts and the noise all but lifted me off the ground. The Wembley finals had huge talent involved including a very prissy, precocious and wonderful Diana Ross; she was a complete star. Others like Gwen Dicky from Rose Royce just froze in front of 76,000 people and we had to physically push her out onto the pitch and just press start on the track.

I did a good job for England rugby and ended up enjoying it a lot. Ultimately, after a good run, the pressures of business and fatherhood took priority, and I resigned from my post. They were incredible times with incredible fans. I had revolutionised the way pre-match entertainment and sports announcements could be in the UK and I'm proud of that.

Back at Wembley, everything carried on between the Twin Towers right up until it closed down and even then, for a couple more years. I went on the road with England playing at Anfield, The Millennium Stadium (for all the domestic Cup Finals), Elland Road, Pride Park and many more. I also went abroad to do the Champions League Final in Paris and once at Old Trafford. I also presided over what many call the greatest Cup Final ever. It was the 2001 UEFA Cup Final, Liverpool v Alavés in Dortmund, Germany.

Liverpool were 3–1 down in the first half and won 5–4. I was sat on the back row of the Liverpool bench and will never forget Phil Thompson, who was assistant to manager Gerald Houllier, going mental for the entire second half.

Two short stories… the only time I lost it on the mic was when David Beckham scored for England to qualify us for the World Cup Finals at Old Trafford. I screamed, and when I was told the result of the Germany game elsewhere, I broke from tradition and announced that we had in fact definitely qualified for the World Cup Finals. The crowd went nuts and the game still had a couple of minutes to play; bad form really, but I got away with it.

We always had guest stars at Wembley. I remember with so much affection being out on the pitch with Norman Wisdom before England's game against Azerbaijan. Norman was a legend in Azerbaijan as well as England and his twisted cap and funny run from the halfway line, falling over and getting up again, was hysterical and the cheer when he scored moved me and him to tears. I've said before that I could fill a book with the Wembley stories, so the last one I will talk about was the most auspicious, nerve-racking and unforgettable one from my ten-year run at our national stadium. Diana, Princess of Wales, died on 31st August 1997, and ten days later, England were to face Moldova at Wembley. The FA got in touch and said that I was going to get to play Elton John's newly-recorded *Candle in the Wind*, which was a tribute to Diana, for the first time at this match. I worked on what to say and the FA tweaked and approved it. On the night, Wembley was sold out and fans laid thousands of flowers around the perimeter of the stadium; the country was still in a state of shock. It was publicised that the song would be played at about 7.50pm and then the strangest thing happened. I started to speak on the mic, "Ladies and Gentlemen, as we all know… " and the entire stadium went completely silent. It caught me by surprise; there were over 74,000 people there and all you could hear was me. I thought the crowd would be able to hear my heart beating; it was so loud it felt like it was beating out of my chest. I didn't fumble and played the song to continued silence. The words lasted about two minutes but it felt like two hours. I looked at everyone around me after I played the CD and they looked back at me with as much relief as I felt. It was exhausting. Later that night, a pal called me to say he was listening to it on the radio and he said they stopped the broadcast to take in my words. It really was, truly, the most surreal moment I had at Wembley Stadium.

Chapter 18

All I Need is Everything

Aztec Camera

Banana Split Productions was firing on all cylinders in the late nineties. Julian, my partner, had made all his money back, plus at least ten times more, and whilst we had a contract now, I felt it wasn't feeling fair anymore. I loved our partnership, but for every one pound I made, I had to give Julian 50 pence and by this time, he wasn't doing anything in practical terms for the business. I know it was the deal but it felt a renegotiation was required. So we went to dinner and I told him how I felt. He said that he was perfectly happy as we stood! No shit, Sherlock, I thought, but if I wanted to buy his shares he was open to an offer. The trouble was, I didn't have any money. I was earning well, but with a growing family everything I earned went on life.

Then one day, just a few short weeks later, a man walked into our offices to discuss his grandson's Barmitzvah with Julian. This man's name was Paul Levinson, I'll never forget him! Looking at my ground floor offices and edit suites, he asked Julian what all this was. Julian, very typically, told him that he had a production company. Paul was a legendary entrepreneur in the entertainment and video business – he had started VCI, one of my biggest clients, and he thought his son-in-law might be interested in the company. Paul's son-in-law was a man called Richard Green and he was the CEO of VCI. I could bore you with a lot of detail now but I won't, suffice to say that nearly a year later, Julian sold all his shares to VCI and I sold half of mine for the same £1m and then I started a VERY long five-year earn-out.

During the lengthy negotiations, there were a couple of times I got very emotional – I just stood up and said, "NO, fuck it, I'm not doing it" and I meant it; they were pushing me too hard. In my emotional naivety, I learnt the best negotiation technique – apathy.

I remember walking out of the lawyer's office after signing the deal. There were about 20 people in there – lawyers upon lawyers, Julian, Nikki was there as a key person, as was my friend, Nicholas Lazarus, who was also a senior member of the team. They were crucial to keep the business growing for my earn-out and needed to sign up for the next five years. If all went well, I could do great out of this. I didn't know it at the time but I completely underestimated how long five years would feel and this would be a great influence on me many years later.

Back to the day itself; I distinctly remember walking out of that office and realising I was a millionaire; I smiled to myself as this was an ambition fulfilled. I think that euphoria lasted about 15 minutes and then I realised that nothing had changed. Work life had to continue in earnest, we had to get bigger and better. When I spoke to the staff the next day, I promised them that nothing would change whilst I was still in charge, and whilst I knew I only owned 26% of the company, as far as I was concerned, I owned 100% and I promised it would feel the same and, in many ways, better. I kept my word.

Very soon after the deal was signed, my new boss, Richard, asked me to take a meeting with his boss, Trevor Bish-Jones, who was the CEO of Woolworths, the owners of VCI at that time. The meet was set for 8.30am and I arrived at 8am to warm the building up a bit as this was early for us. As I arrived, half an hour early, Trevor (who I had not yet met) was sat outside in his chauffeur-driven Jag reading the Financial Times. I couldn't really open up and leave him outside, so I invited him in, made some tea and sat down with my boss's boss. I wanted to be diplomatic so we just chatted about what Banana did and then Richard arrived and went a bit pink as he saw me and his boss chatting… "It's ok," I insisted. "I've not said anything too bad."… Trevor then asked me in front of Richard what I thought of their strategy. I had no idea what he was talking about. "What strategy?" I blurted… Richard went pink again and we bluffed our way through. The truth was, I didn't have a strategy, I wasn't asked for one; I just wanted to get bigger and better doing what we did.

A year later, I was called into VCI's HQ, which is now Soho House in Dean Street, for an HR meeting. I'd never had an HR meeting; I did all the hiring and firing myself. I sat there in this huge boardroom with Richard Green and Jenny Jacobs from HR; she was lovely, but she didn't seem too happy. Richard looked at a sheet in front of him and said, "Steve, you've doubled your staff in a year." Then looking at Jenny, he asked, "Has he done all the paperwork?" Jenny sat with her arms folded, legs crossed and sternly answered, "Nope!" I said, "Oops". Richard then told me that this wasn't right, I had to blah blah blah. I responded, "Richard, I have two massive folders, each five inches thick, full of contracts, do you know what they say? They say, 'make you money'... am I doing that?" "That's not the point," he retorted. "It's exactly the point," I fired back, then looked at Jenny and said, "If you need to do paperwork come down and do paperwork. I'm not an administrator, I'm a creative." They both sighed and left me alone for the next four years... and that's pretty much how my earn-out ran. I was only interested in two things, the company and the work.

I've talked about how this deal felt like fresh air in my lungs. My chest was metaphorically puffed out, and with strong financial backing behind me, I could fight harder, push harder and really go for growth, whilst still doing all the production work we had all grown to love.

Nicholas was a family friend and I had convinced him to join me a couple of years earlier. I needed to pay him a lot of money, more than I have ever paid anyone (including myself); he had a great job at *The Big Breakfast*, but his life was changing. He had just 'come out' after being married and having kids; I thought he was brave and I thought we could work well together. He had loads of cool contacts with the movie studios and he and I started to shoot big movie premieres, LIVE. He produced and I directed. We did some monumental work in this space including all of Tom Cruise's premieres, all the *James Bond* movies, all the *Harry Potters*, in fact we captured 95% of the market. The last *Harry Potter* premiere was in Trafalgar Square and we had 26 cameras, including those on a helicopter, and shot it in 3D for Sky. We were killing it and between us we did over 200 until I had to stop; I was bored of them… Nicholas carried on and today my son Louis does this work and he is better than both me and Nick, along with Richard, who worked for me across Banana and the next company for over 20 years.

A great memory was taking Louis once, aged about 11, to one of the premieres we were doing in Leicester Square. He sat quietly on the floor of the truck as I directed, so quiet I forgot he was there. I was directing away, telling someone to move their camera, they didn't, so I said louder, "Move the fucking camera!" The talkback was open and this little, sweet voice was heard from behind me, "DAD!" It was very funny and all the cameramen were laughing so much that their cameras were shaking. It's so funny to think that Louis is now their boss! At the Odeon that night, I took him to see the stars who were to be presented to the audience. There was a tiny corner, no real backstage area, and we were squeezed in right next to the stars including Morgan Freeman. Louis said louder than he realised, "Dad, it's God!" Morgan had just played God in *Bruce Almighty*; he smiled and ruffled Louis' hair. It was so sweet....

Back at home, I explained to Belinda that the next five years were going to be tough, but if I was able to concentrate on the business, we would come out of it all very well. She understood and was very supportive; she was there at the beginning, helping me to type out the original business plan I had to show Julian and she wasn't giving up on the dream of being comfortable and being able to provide a good education for our kids.

I had to stop the DJ'ing now; this was getting serious and I simply wouldn't have the time. DJ'ing had been very good to me, I had met clients like Coca Cola through my work at Wembley, we kept a roof over our heads thanks to DJ'ing when the mortgages rates went up to over 15%, but it was enough now. I remember one night schlepping to Upton Park to do England v Australia, and I was going to miss my sister-in-law's 30th birthday party. It was cold, wet and miserable and that night, after nearly 13 years, I told the FA I was done. I had stopped doing private parties a few years earlier. I knew what I had to do and I knew it would require focus and determination, along with the full support of my team at Banana and my family at home. All the kids were by now in full-time private education, which was wonderful, and having chosen an office location so close to home, I could whizz home to do bath and bed time. I was now still close enough to take them to school every day and be in the office nice and early. And there were some very funny moments in that office.

During those late night edits, the phone would often ring for London Transport lost property; apparently their phone number was the same as ours but with an 07 as a prefix. As it was late and I thought only someone I knew would ring, I answered the phone with just a "Hello." "Oh, hello there, I left my umbrella on the tube yesterday and wondered if it had been handed in?" "George," I bellowed in a heavy cockney accent, "any umbrellas back there?" I put my hand over the phone and shouted "9,452 – any distinguishing features?" The lady said it had a wooden handle. "6,437 of them," came the muffled response. She hung up. I had to lighten the load during those late-night edits somehow. The number was also confused with the London Transport Help Line, so a big sorry to the gentleman whose bus route to work I cancelled whilst telling him to calm down and not shoot the messenger.

During the day, it could be quite perilous on the phones, like the time Mike Rutherford called and because he was a rock star, the receptionist thought it must be for me. When she announced who the caller was, I immediately presumed it was a particular friend who didn't have the most sophisticated music taste. I picked up the phone and in a super cheery voice said, "Alright Mike? How's Phil?" (Phil Collins, his bandmate). He replied, "I'm sorry? I want to make my daughter a 21st birthday party. Is this the right company?" I quickly said it wasn't and passed him upstairs to Julian's mob.

Productions had now grown in size so much that I needed Julian and his events company to get out of (his) building. We paid him a good rent so he happily fucked off up the road to a new office. During this period, I built 14 edit suites and two sound suites and a TV studio out of a shipping container. Nicholas and I made a TV show called *Celebrity Extra* for five years for Living TV starting in that studio and progressed to make many, many TV shows and movie specials for ITV and Channel 4. I was making more concert specials and the company grew to 55 staff members. I was never happier than walking from edit to edit, keeping my eye on all our creative work and then spending even longer in the sound suite, crafting the sound mixes. Sound is the icing on the production cake and I spent hours and hours in those days stuck in the sound suites, tweaking the mixes and recording voiceovers.

I put a lot of pressure on myself with this earn-out and did everything I could to keep that pressure purely on my shoulders. I didn't want to burden my family or my team at all. I promised the team nothing would change and that the quality of work was paramount; the profitability was my issue, not theirs. Nicholas was my quasi-partner and Nikki, who had been with me virtually from the beginning, was crucial as my producer and lead creative alongside me. I sat Nikki down after the contracts were signed and said that if she stayed with me for the next five years, whatever happened in terms of success, I would give her £100,000; she assured me that I didn't need to, she thought she was well paid and loved her job. Five years later, she came into my office and we both had a good cry when I gave her a cheque for £100,000.

Nikki carried on with me and still works for the next company, Sassy, as I write these memories down.

At this juncture, I do want to mention two instances that happened during my working life as a boss. Both were horrible. I was accused of sexual harassment, of sorts, twice over my 35 years as a boss. To put this into context, that's across hundreds of staff and I think 60% of my team over those years were women. I hired a PA once after my first, Victoria, left to get married and live in the Caymans (Colindale didn't really compete). She was fab and was with me from the get-go. She did accounts, admin, practically everything when we were in our fledgling years. The girl who came in after her was an Aussie; she seemed ok but turned out to be crap so after about three months she just had to go… it happens. Then I received a fax from a firm of lawyers talking of "inappropriate behaviour" etc. Apparently I told her one day that I liked her jumper (I swear) and this made her feel uncomfortable. I was in a meeting with a female client when this fax was put on my desk. I glanced at it and my jaw dropped. I showed my client, Dafina, the letter and she laughed. I called Nikki in and showed her. "OMG," she said, shocked. I was seething, I called my wife and she was shocked as well. All these people knew me well and knew that

I would never intimidate a woman in that fashion, never. It turned out the firm of lawyers she engaged were a cheap 'no-win, no-fee' set up and one response from our lawyers refuting the claims in detail saw the whole thing go away.

My point in telling you this story is to explain how, after being so angry, just how upset I was. I was devastated that my reputation could have been tarnished so early on in my career on the basis of absolute nonsense. This all happened again later in my career at Sassy. The PA in question wrote me a letter complaining about my behaviour. I was so shocked and upset that I handed the letter immediately over to my senior partner, Guy, to deal with. She had used the word 'bullying' and I fucking HATE bullies so I was furious about her allegations. Now, to be clear, I do use fruity language, I'm a creative, we all do, but I use it with a lot of humour. She had been my assistant for maybe two or three years and knew me well. At the time, I was defending keeping her at Sassy to my partners who wanted to get rid of her. So I was doubly upset. She told me that I didn't need to hand the letter over to Guy saying, "Couldn't we just talk about it?" "Sorry, I can't talk to you about this letter," I countered, "I'm struggling to even look at you". Two days later, Guy called me in to his office where our assistant was sat down; she asked to see me alone. I didn't want to but Guy nodded at me as if to say, "Go on". She came into my office and said she was devastated and so sorry about the letter; she'd been having a bad day and had complained to her husband about something I said on the phone to her. HE wrote the letter. She was crying by now; she told me I was the best boss she'd ever had and this had all been a terrible mistake. After such an upsetting incident, there was no way I could work with her anymore and after following HR protocol, we dismissed her. She swore blind to me that she would never sue me and how sorry she was. Three months later, she came after us with lawyers for £10,000. We were just too busy working on positive energy productions to engage in this negativity and wanted her out of our hair so regretfully we paid her. This still pisses me off to this day.

During my last year of the earn-out, I did get lucky with that Ministry fitness video and, after four years of trying, we won all the production work for Woolworths' Christmas TV ads. That was a strange day; I had petitioned from day one to work on these ads, privately it was my secret strategy, but it took me three years and then one day, the acting Marketing Director came to see me and Nikki; it was my last year of the earn-out, so the timing was crucial. Woolworths were with one of the big advertising agencies, BBH. Anyway, he wanted to understand our processes and see if we were up to it. He held up a copy of *The Office* DVD and said he wanted to know how we would advertise it. This was our sweet spot. I asked him for eight minutes; Nikki and I went into her office and wrote the script in five minutes. He thought it was perfect and then wanted to know the price we could offer. Woolies were in trouble and needed to cut costs. We ended up agreeing roughly £2.5k per ad, which was an insanely low cost. However, we got over 200 of the buggers to make in three months and with our internal post facility, it was all gross profit for us at the most crucial time for me.

After I got my final earn-out payment, I said to the group CEO that I was happy to stay on at Banana but he felt they needed to 'cut the cord' and hired someone else to be MD. This didn't work out for anyone except me. This new guy promptly hired me as a creative consultant; he wanted to keep all my relationships live and for the business to keep flowing... nice idea, schmuck! What happened in reality was that over the next two years, during my restricted period, I stayed in touch with all my clients, oversaw work for Banana, got really well paid and had no pressure compared to the previous five years. Also during this period, I was asked to set up a roulette show that would be aired after midnight on ITV; it was easy but so tremendously unfulfilling; I took the money and ran… The minute my two-year restricted period was up, I had a decision to make… what next?

Chapter 19

The Good Life

Frank Sinatra

I had done it! We had money, I had achieved my goals and loved doing what I did along the way; I largely stayed true to my creative principles and my kids were all doing well in private education. The period consulting for my old company was amongst the happiest of my life. I was working for my old company as a creative consultant and the work was easy as I had no true responsibilities. I've always loved working hard and being busy and to do it without the responsibility of keeping every wheel turning is a joy. A by-product of the two-year period of forced 'exile' was that I got to stay in touch with my clients and business friends.

We bought a holiday home in Boca Raton, Florida and

enjoyed many great holidays. There was a golf course there and I had a group of London friends that I played with regularly. The kids would enjoy having a swimming pool, as most young kids would, and I loved it there; it was my happy place. We loved a restaurant called Houstons, which to this day serves the best ribs in the world; a plate of those, coleslaw, skinny fries and a Sea Breeze or two was my go-to meal.

One year early on in our time in Boca, we experienced our first hurricane; well, when I say we, everyone else was asleep, but I was up with my video camera. The day before the Cat 4 storm was due to hit, I spent a back-breaking four hours removing every pebble from my backyard perimeter and putting them all into a very heavy, large dustbin. When the storm hit, of course there wasn't even a rolling stone, let alone one flying through the air and smashing our windows. The water in the house went down and we had to use buckets of water from our overflowing pool to flush the loos. When I eventually ventured out the following morning, I encountered utter devastation. Over 500 massive trees were uprooted and strewn all over the roads; most were blocked. I went round to my mate Stevie A's house to see if everything was ok, it wasn't. His pool was overflowing to the point of being millimetres from coming into his home. I found the tap to open something that relieved the water pressure and saved his home.

We went on great family holidays to other parts of America and I kept working when I wasn't on holiday or playing golf. At home, we decided to move home to my partner Julian's old house just up the road. It was bigger and had a pool; we thought it would be perfect. Julian had separated from his wife, Julie, and Julie and I actually ended up swapping houses, she to mine and us to hers. Both homes suited us and she got the extra money to boot. I'll never forget rolling a giant trampoline up Uphill Road; it was bizarre. We did the house up, which was stressful, as I decided we would keep living there whilst the builders were working. In hindsight, a mistake, but the house ended up looking and being fantastic. I struggled a bit during this time; I had just made over £3m and once we had bought the home in America and done this house swap, there wasn't that much left! The truth was, there was enough, but that's not what my brain was telling me. My brain said – you've just worked your tits off to make a substantial amount of money and now you don't have much cash left at all.

Around about this time, Julian and I invested in a friend and former client of mine; her name was Hasfa and she wanted to sell products via infomercials. It proved to be a good investment. We put her and her team in Julian's offices, I helped make the infomercials and the investment felt solid. Then one day, a couple of years in, she told us both that she wanted to expand and buy a couple of shopping channels. Julian had many wealthy clients and we went to see three of them and a couple I knew, to see if they liked the idea and wanted to invest. All bar one did! We got the money in 72 hrs… We said yes to one of my brother's partners but then one of the others wouldn't lie down easy and he was relentless in pursuing me to go with him. I said we had made our mind up but he would't let it go. His name was Peter and he insisted on lunch with Hasfa and myself so, as he was a good client of mine, we went to pay lip service. Hasfa went to powder her nose towards the end of the meal and when she was gone, he asked me what it would take. I replied matter-of-factly, "Nothing." The other deal was agreed. He countered, "What if I buy you and Julian out?" I said, "How much?" "£1m," he replied. "Agreed," I remarked and held my hand out… of course, it didn't end up being that simple. In fact, like all negotiations, it was mildly torturous. Ultimately, we did sell our shares to Peter and turned a £50,000 investment each into £500,000 each. A good trade as they say….

It's worth pointing out at this stage that this was another deal where I got emotional and told everyone to "Fuck off, I'm not doing this," as they tried to chip us during negotiations. I got up and walked out. Peter came running after me with his big hands on my shoulders telling me it was all part of the fun. It wasn't to me. Anyway, he agreed the point and we got the deal done. You always have to get to a point where you don't give a shit to get a deal done it seems. I got away with it again; the cash was running out and we managed to pull this deal off.

We went on a really nice family holiday to America soon after that, as I'd won a poker tournament and the prize was a trip to Vegas; we brought the kids along and had a lot of fun.

Not yet 40, I was far too young to retire but I didn't feel like I had the gumption to do it all again; maybe I would invest, get an MD or be a Chairman; that felt like a good idea.

Chapter 20

Thank You For The Party

The Dukes

I loved making parties. We had several at 10 Uphill Rd, just BBQs in the back garden with 40-odd friends attending. Naturally, I always wanted entertainment. One year, I remember booking Yeta Rose and Bunny Balloo, two very funny Jewish transvestites. Another year, we had a young Paul Zerdin, before he won *America's Got Talent*; his ventriloquist act is still the best I have ever seen.

During the years of plenty we had some insane parties. Being business partners with probably the best party planner in Europe, if not the world, and still being one of his best friends was a great advantage. I still today can think of no better way of spending hard-earned money than to celebrate with those you love. I'm lucky, I have a lot of friends and so does my middle brother, PK, and a lot of them crossover. Across a six-year period, we Kemsleys had five Bar/Batmitzvahs, two 40th's and our Dad's 70th. These events were a reflection on how both my brother and I think: a) If you are going to do it, do it well, b) Fuck it, you only live once.

Having been somewhat in the party business, there are some crucial rules. When you have a bar, make sure anyone can get any drink they want, that means having every conceivable mixer out there. Whatever you choose as food, try and make it the best version and most importantly, entertain. Admittedly, both me and PK went a little OTT on this last element, but I knew how to book talent, what the right price was and how to make the booking work logistically. For example, when Olly Murs was on tour with JLS and coming off stage in Norwich, I had a car waiting to get him straight to the party to surprise my daughter on the occasion of her Batmitzvah; one of the best moments of my life was seeing Saskia's face at that unique time. I had pretended it wasn't possible and typically she was, "It's ok, Dad, it doesn't matter", but when we brought him out she was instantly crying, which in turn made me cry. If your family loved The Jersey Boys, get the lead singer, Ryan Malloy, over to play a medley of Four Seasons hits and send the crowd crazy. Some bookings were a bit self-indulgent, like having Ben from Curiosity at Joe's Barmitzvah, and ABC at Louis'.

There was a New Year's Eve party we threw in Boca one year; there were a lot of friends and family in town, so we had about 60 people over. I had been making some infomercials in Florida back then, so I used my production team to board over the pool in our tiny backyard and put some lights up and an Elvis lookalike performed. I've told you before that I rarely get drunk, but this night I got smashed on Vodka Red Bulls! I remember waking in the very early hours and asking Belinda why no one had said goodnight to me. I was so drunk that I'd lost three hours of my memory. The next day, I swept up and saw the credit card receipt for the BBQ restaurant that did the catering. I read it and to my horror the bill was $500 and I had tipped them $1,000. I was aghast, and when I drove by the back of the local restaurant later that night on my bike, they all waved in a very cheery fashion… "What's up, Steve? How's your head today man?" they all shouted with huge grins on their faces.

The bookings at our parties were to purely entertain and excite. I was lucky enough to get McFly the week they went to No.1 for Joe, The Sugar Babes were great at Louis' celebration and at my 40th, we had Nick Heyward, DJs Gary Crowley and Greg Edwards, The Pasadenas, comedian Tim Vine and for the finale, Bjorn Again. Extravagant? Yes! Worth it? Abso-fucking-lutely! To see everyone you love having the best time and loving every second yourself is truly a blessing and let's face it, I got all the acts at mates' rates. At my 40th, I used all my contacts to set the studio up like *Top of The Pops*, my lighting team, cameras, staging, it was all within my remit. We had a Yo Sushi conveyor belt and after the party, bacon butties for all. I know I am generous, I know that myself and have been told so many times by loved ones but I am positively tight-arsed and careful compared to my brother, PK. Just before my 40th party, he whisked my (and our) buddies and wives off on a private jet to spend three days and nights on board a super yacht in Sardinia. We had never experienced anything like it, the boat was beyond special. Most of us had never experienced anything so luxurious before. This was the most generous gesture from a brother who was admittedly killing it in the property game.

Around about that time, PK had lost his brother-in-law, Raz, to cancer and that gave him an unparalleled 'live and let live' attitude. PK's 40th was beyond the beyond. About 250 of us got onto a chartered jet and flew to Central Spain where Julian and Banana Split had taken over a resort. What followed has been described amongst us that were there as the peak of the world. The one element that you cannot buy is love, and the love my brother and I had at our parties was so special I can feel it while writing about it. PK had a few acts as well. On night one, the Gypsy Kings performed as we walked into a Spanish hacienda, then up popped the legendary Jackie Mason who was hysterical. Finally to end the night… only a full two-hour set from Billy fucking Joel! PK even duetted brilliantly on *You May Be Right* – mind blown… Day two, everyone was around the pool chilling, there were no kids except for ours which was super special. That night, in a special marquee, I presented PK with a film I made called *PK's World*, with all his most loved ones recorded singing a song at Abbey Road Studios. He sobbed – job done. Later, Craig David performed and to top the night off, Duran Duran blew the roof off. Something unique then happened: one of my brother's wealthy friends gave him a present on stage. The present was the party… "This one's on me, PK," he stated. This gentleman was very successful as you can imagine and wanted to give back, as a couple of years before, PK had made him a 40th as a surprise. He said he nearly had a heart attack when Billy Joel came on....

These were surreal times, we had both worked hard for success and these very private parties were our way of sharing our success with those we loved. I know neither of us regrets a penny or a moment. Of course, doing what I did, there are incredible videos of all these parties to re-live forever. They also took forever to bloody edit. Great memories and happy days and imagine how proud our Mum and Dad were; they still are.

For all of these parties, I would make a special unique film. A tribute to our Dad at his 70th and various others at the kids special parties, all featuring their friends and often pastiching famous songs whilst rewriting the lyrics to personalise them. This was my original idea that I first did at Joe's Barmitzvah. Of course I had a production company and all the post-production facilities so it was a bit of a 'busman's holiday' but they were so fun to do. People then started asking me to produce these films for their special occasions and out of nowhere I had created a mini industry. The budgets got bigger as did the ideas.

I once made a mini comedy movie starring Simon Cowell, Kate Moss, Kelly Brook and many more for a good budget. These films were creatively inspiring and of course the clients left all the imagination to me and I was let loose. Plus, I often had the joy of watching an audience enjoy these films first-hand and that's a feeling one didn't often get in my business. To this day, despite the many commercial success my films had, I think I had the best of times making these unique mini-movies.

Another absolute favourite was re-imagining *Oliver!* with costumes and amazing sets to boot. Over the years, I produced loads of these 'private films' including pastiches of *Hamilton*, *Hairspray*, *Moulin Rouge*, countless classic pop songs including *Bohemian Rhapsody* and loyal generous clients gave me budgets that enabled us to excel in all of these productions. I had full creative freedom and they were among the best and most fun productions I have created over the years, bizarrely for the smallest audiences. Looking back, it's nice to think that I created a genre that still lives on today, although I think I had the best of the budgets.

As a footnote, at this point I need to point out (somewhat weirdly) that I hate body odour! There is no excuse for it, there is no need to stink; what could be worse than a stinky waiter leaning over you as you are about to eat, or an editor that you have to spend several hours with in an enclosed room stinking like he hasn't washed in a week? I have, in my life, had to confront these issues in a major way. I gathered all the waiters at Sassy's Batmitzvah, having sent someone out to buy cans of deodorant and explained that, to smell tonight was unacceptable to me and please, all of you, go around the corner and have a good long spray. I remember an editor and a graphics person at Banana who also stunk, in one case I think it was just damp laundry, either way it had to stop, so both times I gathered the whole company to explain my views on personal hygiene. Only Nikki knew who I was really talking to.

Chapter 21

Sassy

Neneh Cherry

By now, I had moved back into Julian's new Banana Split office to carry on consultancy with my old company and work out what I wanted to do next. I did interview a potential MD for any future venture; I spent two hours with her, spilling my guts and at the end of the meeting she told me she was going over the road to meet with my old company, Banana Split. WTAF? I'm not doing this anymore, I couldn't trust anyone... this lady went on to buy Banana, so if I was to go again, I'd have to do it myself and frankly what I told her still had to be actioned. She managed to quickly reduce Banana from a team of 55 to 5, so bollocks to her.

I liked being back with Julian; he wrote bad emails

and I enjoyed correcting his grammar and he was and still is a great sounding board for me. Julian is so different to me in so many ways but, when it comes to business thinking, we are like brothers and he is still today my emergency contact in my passport. I'm not sure there is anyone I trust more to get something done. When my old company Banana 'cut the chord' and I got the job as creative consultant they said I had to form a company in order to invoice them. I had 24 hours and came up with Sassy Films, obviously named after Saskia, who I call Sassy. Were the boys jealous? I don't think so; Joe Films and Louis Films didn't have the same ring and Sassy is an adjective! In those days, the word 'sassy' wasn't used at all in Europe; it was essentially an American phrase. People thought we were in the porn business at first. The original logo was my hand-drawn version which is still probably my favourite one.

Towards the end of my two-year 'gardening leave' I was driving around looking for a potential office for the future. There was an embryonic business park in Elstree. Elstree was the home of TV and Film in the UK and twinned with Hollywood; it was a sign. There were a couple of units I liked, one was double the size of the other and I was not fully engaged in the idea of going again and going for growth, versus a lifestyle business. I called my brother, PK, who was a phenomenal risk-taking property entrepreneur, and my very close friend, Giles, who was my builder, and they both said I should go for the big one. Giles would get the work, so of course, he said double the size and PK was always aggressive in his business thinking so it was always going to be a bigger property in his opinion. Then I remembered some advice I got from a client many years earlier when I quizzed him on the secrets of his success. Peter was in the coat hanger business (I kid you not) and he thought space was key; he told me if one had space one could grow… I went for the double unit.

Now how would I fund it? I still had some money but by no means enough to splash out £1m so I approached my bank manager at Coutts. My bank manager was brilliant, her name was Sasha Speed; I had met her a year earlier in Cannes at MIPCOM. I already had a Coutts business account thanks to Julian but she was a private banker. I wasn't even sure what that meant but she explained it was a personal account for me and nothing to do with my business. I wanted one of those. I was still with Barclays in Harrow on the Hill from when I was 14, so it felt appropriate that now I actually had some money I should have a 'grown up' account. Sasha signed me up and was great at explaining to my ADD brain what was required and when. Coutts were ingrained in the creative community and she was an entertainment specialist so I thought she would have great contacts. Fast forward two years, I called her to ask how she thought I could fund this property. I needed £657,000 and she just offered to lend me the money over a five-year period. I couldn't get a mortgage on a commercial property with a new business so this was kind of my only route. Funding property was not my space, it was 2006 and everything was looking good. I signed the deal with Sasha and bought the building all within a four-week period. Giles came in and we spent a pile on doing the building up – we added a mezzanine floor, built a proper TV studio (always a dream of mine) and I built six edit suites without thinking too much; it seemed I was doing it all again. I do remember the words, "stick to what you know" ringing in my brain. It seemed all the good senior guys at Banana wanted to rejoin me; they weren't happy. Nicholas would come over and this time I offered him a partnership as he had a bunch of good clients, Nikki would come, along with Richard and a few others. My restrictive covenants were done with and before I knew it we had 21 staff and we were very much back in the saddle.

My biggest old client from Banana were De Agostini and I had breakfast with James, their Marketing Director. I told him that we were going again, starting Sassy and would he still like us (me and Nikki) to still make his ads. Not only did he say yes, but when I explained how tough the first few months' cashflow would be and would he be ok paying 50% in advance of the first ad, he said there would be two ads and he would pay fully in advance of production on both of them. To this day, this is the kindest gesture I had ever had from a client. We were off... I loved the building as I got to design it from scratch and the vibe was fantastic. I had funded the business 100% and gifted Nicholas 10%. Nikki decided she didn't want shares or any great corporate responsibility; she just wanted to carry on working in a cool creative environment with me and then it was 2008 and the phones stopped ringing!

Chapter 22

Trouble in Paradise

Al Jarreau

As many of you will recall, in 2008, there was a financial crisis, and for me it was my first since being in business. I had handled the first one whilst at Diamond Time by DJ'ing more and eating beans on toast; this was different. I had just reinvested all the money I had made selling Banana in a building for the new business, a new home in Mill Hill, a home in America and setting up the infrastructure and cashflow of Sassy Films. The same entrepreneur who, many years earlier, told me to go for more space also more recently told me that it was a lot tougher having money and losing it than it was to build from nothing and end up back at nothing. I was about to learn that lesson first-hand, or was I? I guess the phones, in hindsight, didn't really stop ringing overnight, but it felt like that to me. Nicholas' side of things was going fine, we had the American movie studios still doing premieres and we had work in production, the team were what I would call medium busy, but it simply felt quiet to me. I always ran my businesses on gut instinct and my gut wasn't happy! I found myself working furiously in the morning and then by about 2pm, twiddling my thumbs. This had never happened to me, I had persistently been full-on busy for nearly two decades, so my brain started catastrophising. I would fall asleep at about 11pm and, without fail, wake up at 4 am; the second I woke up, I started to worry, my tummy went into tumble dry spin mode. What had I done? I had money and now I'd blown it all on a fabulous home, starting again and a fantastic building to house a team who weren't going to be busy enough to keep the business afloat. It was all my own money, I had no backing. I would run on the treadmill in our home gym thinking I could use my Range Rover and do executive driving, but would that cover the mortgage payments? The school fees? This went on for months. Belinda wasn't sympathetic; I remember distinctly her telling me to "grow some balls", not what I needed right then. I'm sure there were also words of encouragement but I think the fear I was feeling transferred to her and she didn't like it. I didn't like it either.

I had always smoked weed with a little tobacco since I was 16 or so. I decided to stop for three months to see if that would help me sleep, it didn't. This wasn't good. I would still get up, go to the gym and go into the office but those quiet afternoons were killers. One day, I went to my best mate Michael's office and offered to sell him and another friend who was in business with Mike half my business for £100k, just to tide me over. Both Michaels looked at me as if I was nuts. What was I talking about? My business was worth way more than that, my head wasn't working right. I went to the doctors after six months feeling like my world was imploding; within weeks, I had a Professor of Psychology prescribing pills, a CBT therapist and a regular shrink. The pills, my friends told me, 'monged me out', my outgoing personality was working at 50% maximum but I was determined to fight and get better. I don't remember any eureka moment but after about a year of this, I started to wean myself off the drugs, the CBT was a bit pants and the therapy mildly useful (therapy would become much more important to me later in life).

Looking back now, this truly was a shit time. I didn't feel supported at home. At work I was supposed to be the lifeblood of the business; everyone looked to me for encouragement and support. I simply wasn't able to provide it to the best of my ability. I now call this my 'dark year' and firmly believe in the old adage, "That which doesn't kill you only makes you stronger." The experience gave me a great understanding of mental health before it rose into the general consciousness of most.

Thereafter I was able to talk to my staff with empathy and not only recommend but often pay for my team to visit my osteopath, Dominic, a true life (or back) saver, but also to recommend therapy where appropriate and fund it. I've done this many times for staff and friends over the years; it's a great gift for me to be able to help. I was never one for just giving money; if I am going to help anyone, I always want it to be practical help.

During this melee, and because his part of the business seemed to be chugging along nicely, I promised Nicholas another 10% shareholding, so now we were 80/20. We earned the same wages and I was ok with the deal; understandably, so was he.

As the financial crisis eased, so the phones started ringing again, but there was collateral damage; I had to make 7 of our 21 staff redundant and that was just awful. I'll never forget thinking that I would have to do all my PA's work myself, so she would have to go. Her name was Jo and I liked her a lot, but I was simply on auto-pilot trying to keep the business afloat. By the end of the crisis, I wanted to hire five of the seven back. Some came back, some had found other roles, but Jo was angry and very upset with me. I hate to say it, but I would make the same decision again today. The business had to come before my own well-being and I could not just employ someone because they made my life easier. It got tough and the tough had to keep going… sorry, Jo, you were a great assistant. We are fine now and have spoken a few times over the years, but she was so upset which, in turn, really upset me.

Chapter 23

Your Kisses Are Charity

Culture Club

In the Jewish community, charity is a big deal and as I have mentioned, I've never been one to just give money; I always want to give a bit more, be practical. One day, a very close friend of mine, who I call Stevie A, formed a charity called Rays of Sunshine – it was a children's charity providing wishes for terminally ill or seriously ill kids. Steve asked me to make a fundraising film for them, and I loved the idea of putting our creative talent and practical resources to use in this way. I decided to take on the film personally – I wanted to write, produce and direct. This was a truly worthwhile cause and as I'd spent so many years producing frivolous entertainment, this felt like a nice thing to do. The film was a phenomenal success. I carried on making

Rays' films for over 20 years and produced many, many films for other charities like Norwood, Future Dreams, Cancer Research and the Holocaust Educational Trust. HET was a weird one; Nick and I pitched for it one year and I became very passionate very quickly about the subject matter. I had a great idea but we didn't win the work. WTF? I was pissed off, so we went back again the next year. I won the work, made the film which raised record amounts of money and for the last 12+ years have produced HET's films every year. It's one of my favourite charities. I have met and interviewed over 40 Holocaust survivors, a substantial percentage of whom have now passed but we have their testimonies and they will live on forever in our films.

One year, I made Rays' and HET's films and was also asked to produce a film for Grief Encounter. Grief Encounter was particularly tough to make because of the subject matter. I met and interviewed six families that had lost someone close to them, in many cases a young parent, a spouse and in some instances a brother or sister. This was emotionally hard work and exhausting. When I make these films, I like to go it alone, sometimes operating the camera myself, often viewing all the rushes and creating a paper edit and then working with an editor on every part of the post-production. I become immersed in the process, which means the charity has to put a lot of trust in me as I don't like too much interference until I have finished my 'director's cut'. The relationships I now have with these charities are so strong that the trust is implicit and we have found an amazing way to work together on these films every year.

There was one time however when I made what I consider to be one of the best films I have made for a charity called Jewish Care. I shot on 16mm film in old age homes across London and the home counties. I spent hours creating moving captions to highlight spoken words that were essentially the script. I worked well with the charity's representative and knew the film would have to be approved by the 'committee'. I was so proud of the work and insisted on presenting it personally to the 12-person committee of which my old partner, Julian, was a part of. We all sat in an opulent boardroom in the West End and I played the film. Everyone watched in silence except one lady who kept making notes on her pad. As she made her notes, her many bracelets jangled and she constantly took her eyes off the film to write. I was miffed at first but by the end I was furious, steaming! As the film ended, the room fell silent, everyone exhaled; to me this is the best reaction I could have hoped for. The chairperson enthused, "Wow, that was very powerful indeed," and asked if there were any thoughts from the assembled hierarchy and everyone nodded that they agreed and thought it was perfect, except jangly bracelet lady who, referring to her fucking notes, said she wasn't sure about the moving words (the animated captions, Twat Features, I thought). The rest of the committee mumbled that they quite liked them. I had spent hours and hours on those captions so I said, quick as a flash, "Fine, you can take them off but then you can't show the film." "What do you mean?" snapped jangly lady. "Exactly what I just said," and repeated myself in a very terse voice. Julian sunk down in his chair with a 'fucking hell' look on his face; he knew when I was angry. The chairperson said she thought there would be no need for that and the film worked. It raised £7m a week later, the largest amount any film I have made has raised in one night. I wasn't invited back to produce the next year though.

I have always stated that when producing this work you have to pull up the 'emotional drawbridge'; you can't allow yourself to become emotional until the film is made and then I often weep in the edit suite alone. After a shoot with a bereaved family, a terminally ill child, or an emotional Holocaust survivor, I was always physically exhausted The mental exhaustion transmutes to the physical for me, I think it's for my mental self-protection. I have to remain calm and focused when doing these interviews and often the subjects get emotional. There is one exception to this rule. I made a film for a breast cancer charity called *Future Dreams*, their first. The charity was run by a dynamic mother and daughter combo, Sylvia Henry and Danielle Leslie. They were formidable, Dan was a good friend as our children schooled together and her husband, Spencer, is a great friend too. Dan and Sylvie used to argue a lot in the edit suite with me; it was funny, they clearly adored each other, and during production of this first of many films, I had to film Sylvie receiving chemotherapy, which was both a privilege that she would let me film such a personal process but at the same time quite difficult. I completed the film and many subsequent ones. Sylvia lost her battle with secondary breast cancer and then a year later, Dan would discover she too had secondary breast cancer. Those close knew what this meant. Danielle called me one day and asked me if I'd be willing to film some messages she wanted to record for her children, husband and those closest to her. I knew immediately what this meant and said I would come over that week. She was quite unwell by now and I knew this assignment was going to be tough. Time for that 'emotional drawbridge' I thought. No chance!! What happened that afternoon was simply remarkable. With no notes and absolute confidence and self-control, Dan just spoke to everyone she loved via my camera. I knew I had to do it personally; with no sound recordist and no camera operator, I sat and tried to ensure the sound levels were right and everything was at least in focus. I sat there for hours just leaking from my eyes and nose quietly to myself, just the two of us. I was privy to the most intimate private messages and it was utterly draining. Danielle however was completely stoic despite the subject matter. I had to stop her after about half an hour to get tissues, for me! She huffed in frustration, in a playful way and we completed the task. After Danielle passed, I created a private DVD for each family member and close friend; there were over 14. I will never produce work tougher than that; it was by far the best and worst job of my life. Two remarkable women so dearly missed today over 15 years later.

I have made films to raise awareness of political situations in the middle east on more than one occasion but the one worth mentioning was when I had to interview Tony Blair who was by then the UK governments middle east envoy. I took my eldest son

Joe to the shoot and he recalls the ex prime minister having the firmest handshake he has, to this day, ever experienced. I remember when interviewing Mr Blair on camera feeling like I could see his master diplomatic brain whirring at each question and delivering answers that were so perfectly balanced, when I was looking for more controversy or bias in my clients favour. Not a chance Kemsley this one knows what he is doing.

I have conservatively worked out that the films I have produced over a 17-year period have raised well over £50m and that's what I mean by practical help. I was also once invited by the Rays of Sunshine charity to attend a tea at Number 10 Downing Street. What a buzz getting in a black cab with my friend, Spencer, and saying, "Number 10 Downing Street please, guvnor!"

Chapter 24

Brothers in Arms

Dire Straits

I'm going to take a chapter to move away from the almost chronological story and talk about my brothers. The truth is, just like Wembley, this could be a book on its own. As you have discovered throughout this book, I have two brothers, Paul (now better known as PK) and Andrew. PK is two years my younger and Andrew four. Where do I begin?

Growing up, it all felt so normal. I remember thinking that we are so normal, we even used normal shampoo (as opposed to that for greasy or dry hair); this was an absolute thought process when we lived in Hatch End. We did normal stuff; we ate Mum's shit homemade hamburgers, and were starved of treats to the point of having to steal chocolate biscuits at five in the morning by clambering up onto a perilous kitchen unit and, on tiptoes, reaching into the cookie jar, only to be caught in the act. Dad installed a pay phone, I swear, a pay phone, weirdo. I really don't remember having much to do with my brothers other than everything we did as a family. Being older, I did my own thing. I did once have Paul on my shoulders, horsing around, which resulted in chipped teeth, masses of blood, tea towels and hospitals when he fell chin-first onto the corner of our coffee table. Poor sod ended up with gold teeth before the rap generation. Andrew didn't feature much at all in my younger life, as I said, apart from when we were all together as a family unit, but let's not forget this all falls into the part of my life that holds very few memories for me.

As we grew up, I think we all got kind of closer and had more in common. Certainly PK and I now share many friends. Andrew started a career in hospitality at TGI Friday's, he had some nice friends and girlfriends and was particularly close to Mum. When Belinda and I first had our boys, Joe and Louis, Andrew used to come over a lot to play with them, often taking them out. It was all good, until it wasn't.

Andrew met his now-wife of over 20 years, Lisa, and

we were all happy for him, but something went wrong and this is my view, cos it's my book... Lisa was a strong woman, her mother was even stronger and during the planning of the wedding, she had definite views on what she wanted. Despite having six young nieces and nephews, there were to be no page boys or girls. This was a shame and I think it upset a few of the Kemsley women. PK and I had done well by now and we were pretty generous with the wedding gifts and many have suggested that what was to follow was due to jealousy; I do not believe this to be the case. Ultimately, Lisa just felt shunned by the Kemsley women: my wife, PK's wife and our Mum. I don't believe her feelings were fully justified but what then happened, for me, is so, so wrong on so many levels. Andrew stopped talking to all of us, including his Mum and Dad (that's the so, so wrong bit). They were very close. What had happened for him to shun his whole family, the kids as well? I tried to keep the lines of communication open and, for a couple of years, spoke with Andrew every now and then to try and get him to talk to our parents. Belinda wrote letters, we went round to their flat when they had their first child but Lisa was, and by all accounts still is, a fortress. Perhaps she had her man and no one else was allowed to share? She sent birthday cards back to my Mum with a note saying, "I don't know what you hoped to achieve by sending this"; who the fuck does that? I have no ill feelings to Andrew as it doesn't bother me that much, I'm just sad for Mum and Dad, they have written letters, cousins have tried to make *shalom* (peace). Once at an Auntie's funeral, Andrew turned up and slipped his arm into Mum's as we walked from the grave. She cried, saying to him, "I'm still your mum." He replied, "I'm still your son." There was hope… then nothing.

It's a bizarre thing that for over twenty years, Andrew has not been part of any of our lives; even when Dad got really, really sick, he stayed away. I've only seen him at funerals and shivas and we are always civil but he has missed out on so much, as have we all – all those family celebrations – and his two children don't know any of their six cousins or their grandparents on our side. If pressed to answer as to why, I would say simply that Andrew is weak and Lisa is very strong, not that being strong is a bad thing, it's probably perfect for Andrew. All I do know for sure is that the combination has led to misery for my parents and that makes me sad.

Now PK, WTAF, he changed his monocle to PK after moving to America for a slight reinvention. Paul was always a unique child. If I left a wet towel on the floor

I was told to pick it up, but in Paul's case, Mum picked it up and metaphorically that's how it's been his whole life. His first wife used to tell tales of baths overflowing and wet towels everywhere. Paul was my little brother, two years my junior, and if I saw him in school, I would always look out for him. I've been defending him my whole life and always will as he truly does have a heart of gold and is literally generous to a fault! I believe my success at such a young age was an inspiration of sorts for Paul, but his success put mine in the shade; if I thought I was ambitious, he made me look like a plodder. He didn't excel in academia and became an estate agent at about 17 – what happened in the next 15 years was nothing short of insane. He built a business worth over half a billion pounds; the problem was, he wouldn't stop, he wanted a billion! He lived like a billionaire, made friends with billionaires, flew privately all over the world, even buying a private jet once with a business partner. He was vice-chairman of Tottenham Hotspur FC, became a little famous by being a regular on Alan Sugar's *The Apprentice* and was larger than life. He has given millions to charity, he's been up to all sorts in Vegas (I never went on those trips, they scared me) but as fierce as he was and still is, I have been able to be his objective advisor in matters of the heart or when the shit really hits the fan. I'm his big bro and I'm proud of him on so many levels. I maintain that if I was his chairman over the years that half a billion might have made it to a billion, as I would have nicked half the chips off the table and made him play with the other half, not only in the casinos of the world but also in life. That's just not the way he rolled or even how he still rolls today. I might say, "Look after the pennies and the pounds will look after themselves", he might say, "Fuck the pennies." He was an incredible gambler.

I once made a video for his eldest son Daniel's Barmitzvah, it was Paul's idea and I somehow pulled it off. It was an almost impossible 360-degree animation based on live-action filming with 360-degree audio. It took three months to produce and blew the crowd away. Anyway, he went to the casino the night I said I needed the money paying and he gave me the largest amount of cash I had ever seen the next day after a big win. He's won millions and lost millions. There are so many PK stories, but I should leave them for his book. Bottom line: he is the only brother I have contact with and we remain close today. He is frustrating and he is wonderful, perhaps even wonderfully frustrating. He loves me and mine and he loves our Mum and Dad. What else could one ask for… maybe a bit of stability, but I'm not sure if that will ever happen. He married for the second time to Dorit, one of the *Real Housewives of Beverly Hills* and has two more wonderful kids, five in all, and I love them all. He hasn't got everything right in his life, but essentially he is one of the good guys and he is my brother so don't fuck with him or you'll have me to answer to!

Chapter 25

All Night Long

Lionel Ritchie

I wanted to write a chapter on some of the insane filming projects I have undertaken thanks to my partner, Julian. After the experience of the Saudi Prince, private parties were fun but bloody hard work. The hours were uncompromising, we had to film the builds, the set-ups and right up to when the guests left the parties. My crew were not used to these hours and we were often in sunny/sunburn places, so the budgets had to be substantial.

In the early days, my friend, a well-known DJ, was to marry a lovely lady whose father was very wealthy. Now, wealthy people are not fools and hate paying more just because they are rich. The negotiations for this wedding video took two weeks and involved lots of chicken and rice, the dad driving in his Rolls Royce on the wrong side of the road and ultimately, a tough, long shoot. I swore after that job I would never do a wedding video again! About 20 years later, I broke my promise to myself, and got involved in a wedding film that was to be shot over three days in Los Angeles; it sounded fun, and I got to make a pop video pastiching Bruno Mars' *Marry You* with people like Jimmy Carr and my golfing buddy, Vernon Kaye. The biggest satisfaction I have always had in my career is being in a room with an audience seeing one of my films. The reactions and compliments are amongst the greatest joys of my working life. Guests at the first night's party of that LA wedding included Elton John and to see the reactions to this video being played on a giant screen was humbling and deeply satisfying. The wedding shoot itself was, as expected, gruelling but the results of the work that Julian did at those events were spectacular. Honestly, there have been many occasions at the end of one of those shoots where I simply couldn't feel my feet or walk when I finally crashed at the end of the night. Let's also be honest, to be at these parties and stay in some of the best hotels in the world was a privilege. However, by far the greatest joy from this, my second and last fee-paying wedding video, was watching the film with the bride and groom in their private cinema in London several weeks later. He was and still is a tough businessman; what a joy that, after the three of us watched it, without interruption, we all sat in our respective seats wiping tears from our eyes. They also didn't change a frame. The same happened when I filmed *PK40*; we all sat down to watch nearly three hours of film that took months to edit and all my brother said was, "You nailed it, Stevie." This is satisfying work and I knew I was good at it.

I remember being in the South of France filming for the nicest billionaire I've ever known, and another very successful entrepreneur came up behind me when Stevie Wonder came on, and whispered in my ear, "It's become a pissing competition, I'm getting out." Yeah, right, I thought.

A couple of years later, this man threw the greatest wedding party I have ever filmed (he dragged me back in). At this party, inside London's famous Roundhouse, Posner the party king built an entire rainforest, not an inch of that famous venue was not dressed in foliage, there was a 25-foot high waterfall, a wall of rocks with naked men and women painted into it. It was insane! Elton John was the main act and he appeared out of the middle of a giant hydraulic tree, but by far the most amazing bit was when Elton sang *Circle of Life* – Julian got the entire theatre cast of *The Lion King* to enter as they do at the beginning of the show, with all the flying mannequins of animals, completely in the round. It was spectacular Posner and made for a great film. I have filmed Elton live three times over the years and made a pop video with him and Blue. He is a pro, a bit grumpy sometimes, but always the consummate professional.

The part I love about these parties is the live acts. When I worked with Julian on a daily basis, I was instrumental in the booking of some of these acts, some I knew and recommended to Julian, like Joan Rivers, who 'tore the house down' once at a party in the Maldives. Another time, in the early days of Banana, I knew the people involved with Bros and Julian had a young kids' party in London for a very prominent, ridiculously wealthy, sovereign leader. I offered Bros £200,000 in 1989 to take two hours, including travel time, away from their rehearsals for their upcoming show at Wembley Stadium to play at the party. £200k is worth £500k today! They were the biggest pop act in the UK at that moment and they said no! Oh well, they might have regretted that a few short years later… if they ever knew about it personally.

To film acts like Stevie Wonder, Rod Stewart, Robbie Williams, Michael Bublé, Bruno Mars, Michael Jackson, Beyoncé, George Michael and about 50 others was a thrill and part of the reason I loved my job. Julian did parties all over the world and I filmed all the big ones. Jobs in the Maldives, hanging out of helicopters on the Côte d'Azur; It doesn't sound like it but this was tough work and I was twice the price of my competitors, but our product was twice as good. It's worth pointing out that in those days, the cameras and media was a lot heavier and cumbersome than those of today. Today, they can film on light rigs with drones. It was always the post-production (editing) that I spent months on. I was frame accurate when I worked on this stuff and my music choices were key; once a DJ….

There are two specific stories that I'd like to tell; the first is when I was hired to make a 'movie' to play at one of these such parties. It was a film of the host's life but conceived as a black comedy. My client commissioned the script that we ended up writing in-house and then the filming took a few weeks in London, LA and the South of France. I searched for experienced and award-winning people to help me but at every stage I got rid of them and we ended up doing it all ourselves. The casting, the writing, producing and I directed. We had stars like Kate Moss, Simon Cowell and real actors playing real-life people who would be in the room the night the film was to be shown. The film ended up being about 25 minutes long. I was thrilled with it, as was my client, and on the night, it went down unbelievably well. I always tell the story of being introduced to Leonardo DiCaprio as the man who made that film and him giving me a high five, telling me with a genuine giant grin that he thought it was "fucking awesome man". That was why I did this work. To be in the room to see the reactions is still a great thrill. Today, I often go to cinemas to see the concerts we film for cinema release just to see the fan reactions. I have mentioned probably 10% of the private work I have been involved with over the years and there are so many more stories, but I happen to know Julian wants to write his book, so I'll leave them to him. Julian, don't forget to mention the massive party in St Petersburg, Russia in the freezing snow with President Bill Clinton in attendance and the incredible Tina Turner and Elton John in concert. What a film that made. The funniest part for me at this job was that all my crew and I had to wear traditional 18th century costumes. I was the last to get fitted and they ran out of staff costumes. I couldn't be in the palace ballroom in jeans so they got me a costume from the

Palace Museum that they said was insured for over £100,000, it was so fucking heavy but I felt quite the Disney Prince in it.

The last one I'll mention here is my George Michael story… George was my favourite artist; I was a big fan, his talent blew me away, One night, he was due to play a full concert in the Maldives and because I knew his personal security of thirty years, Ronnie, I was allowed on stage to get those key reverse shots, my favourite shots. After the party, Ronnie, who was my friend, asked me if I knew anyone with a joint for George. "Me," I replied, and despatched Ronnie off to my room at the other end of the island with my safe code to retrieve the tiny bit of weed I had. Ronnie came back about half an hour later telling me he'd found the room but had forgotten the safe code. We laughed and I told him, "Come on, I'm done here now." In the golf buggy he said that I should come back and have a smoke with George… ok I thought, why not?

Back at George's villa, I let him roll the joint (big mistake); he was a bigger smoker than me and put three times the amount in than I would have. I don't like being stoned and really just smoke out of habit and as a way of chilling. George and I chatted as

I smoked with him. Then I felt what is commonly known as a 'whitey' coming on; I was mullered. What I haven't mentioned is that I was dressed in a full length, almost transparent silk skirt, a silk waist jacket, traditional Maldivian costume as dictated by the night's dress code. Here I was, chatting and smoking with one of my heroes, and my head was beginning to spin. I quickly made my excuses and slowly shuffled out in my skirt. The next day, when George left the lunch, he sought me out for a handshake and to say thank you, but what he and I didn't know at this point was that we were going to meet again soon.

A few months before this party, and feeling flush after selling my first business, we were invited to a Terence Higgins Trust auction by my friend, Billy Sammeth. Billy knew I was a George fan and told me that every year in this private space, Kenny, George's partner, auctioned dinner with George for the charity. Billy told me it always went for a couple of grand, so I attended with the sole purpose of getting that dinner with my favourite singer.

By the time the auction was underway, Belinda had downed a glass or two of champagne, I was driving: I wanted her to do the bidding, as I knew people in the room including George's manager and assistant, and I didn't want them knowing it was me trying to buy the dinner. Belinda sat in front of me, having not eaten much, and definitely tipsy. "Go up to two grand," I told her… there were four guys on the front row jointly bidding against us and knowing how much I wanted the dinner, Belinda just kept bidding. It went up to £10,000 and I had to grab both her arms to stop any more action.

After we thankfully failed in our bidding attempts, I went and said hello to Michelle, George's assistant, as I had being dealing with her on the Geri Halliwell videos. I casually mentioned I was trying to get that dinner and she told Kenny. Kenny instantly said he would do another dinner if I matched the bid. What was a man to do? Nearly a year later, after much to-ing and fro-ing over dates, we met George and Kenny in a very smart Japanese restaurant in St James in London. Coincidentally, it was a few weeks after the Maldives. All I'll say is that we were the last four people in the restaurant that night as they were putting chairs on the other tables. We spent over four hours chatting and drinking sake (we got a cab). George asked me to come to his Christmas Party, but we were going to be in America, so I politely had to decline. I had my moments with George and felt privileged to get to know him a bit. When George died on Christmas Day in 2016, I was gutted and angry; he had so much more to give the world. His demons won and we were all robbed of the greatest talent of our generation.

Chapter 26

Back to Life

Soul II Soul

The financial crisis was done with, my mental health was back to full fitness, and I was ready to get the business back to its full potential. I had a risky business model, I was totally self-funded, all the capital expenditure was mine – the studios, the edit, sound and graphics suites – and unlike the vast majority of production companies, I wanted full-time staff. It gave us creative flexibility. If we needed to spend more time in the studio or edit, it didn't cost more cash, it only used more overhead, but that overhead was substantial – nearly £400k a month – so we simply had to be busy or we would lose money, but if we *were* busy we would make money. Not rocket science but risky nonetheless.

The problem was I was the main rainmaker, along with Nicholas. He brought in roughly £1.5m and I had to bring in £3.5m; it was getting harder as I got older. There is definitely a period in an entrepreneur's life where they will have maximum energy; I was getting nearer to my 50s and felt we needed more help and at a senior level. I had a bright but mostly young team who were always, as instructed by me, asking lots of questions. It's been a mantra of mine, "He who asks the most, learns the most" and is often the cleverest in the room. Often in meetings, I would stop someone and ask them what they meant. Nothing drives me madder in business than the use of acronyms. So often, people use them and when I ask what they mean, they never bloody know. I digress… I knew we needed more senior people and I would never be able to sell for a second time if it was all about me. Enter Guy. Guy was previously a client at Living TV and Nicholas thought we should meet up. Guy recalls not being sure about me at all but decided to give it a go. I thought he could be a good COO type but insisted he sat up in the big open-plan production office as he came from media and didn't necessarily know about production. He told me years later that he used to go home in those early days and say to his wife, Jo, that he really didn't think it was going to work out and that I was a bit much. Well, today Guy is a part-owner of Sassy Films, so he was wrong….

We knew Channel 4 and over the years had made many TV programmes for them, including a film review series, but Guy knew the commercial team and that turned out to be a very good thing. Channel 4 ended up using Sassy to come up with advertising ideas to sell into potential big brands for sponsorship idents (the mini-adverts just before a programme starts or the commercial break happens) and we would make those idents; we also created many one-off bigger budget TV commercials. We enjoyed the work except, at times, having to deal with the incumbent big advertising company; that was always painful and often Guy or Nikki would keep me away from some of these meetings. You know, the sort of meeting where to make a tiny decision, 18 wankers sit around a table musing their university-educated tiny minds about a font size.

My personality was too strong for these meetings and Guy had more patience and knew how the game worked. I had spent my entire career developing a business model that was the complete antithesis of this way of working. Previously, we went to brands, said yes, gave them a budget and got on with it. We delivered TV spots for £150k that an agency would charge £500k for, so keeping me and them apart was probably sensible. Slowly but surely, Guy bought into the company and learnt the business, he offered sensible working practises and ultimately wanted bigger ticket productions and clients. Fine, go for it, Guy.

One little story that features Guy and me… Guy is not Jewish and had never been to Israel. We had a client called Soda Stream; I directed all their work at the time and we were called to a meeting in Tel Aviv. We flew out on EasyJet which was ok, the passengers were a real 'mishmash' of sorts. However, the next day, after the meet, we were to get the late night flight back to Luton with EasyJet. I knew what we were about to witness, Guy had no clue. The plane was full – and I mean 98% – of what we call "frummers", the ultra-Orthodox Jews with the hats, the *payers* (curly bits) and the women in *sheitals* (wigs). We tried boarding the plane quickly as they all pushed into our speedy boarding lane and the mayhem had begun. All of them, up and down the plane, sharing food, orange squash, saying prayers, it was madness. Guy had never seen anything like it. There were about five of us in this one row who were secular. The pilot asked twice for everyone to sit down as we needed to take off. The senior stewards then had a go, saying we were going to miss our slot. I lost it! I fucking lost it! I stood up, and as loud as I could possibly shout (which is very loud) screamed, "SIT DOWN, ALL OF YOU. IT'S NOT COMPLICATED, JUST BEND YOUR KNEES AND SIT!" I cannot fully explain how loud I was, but the whole plane fell silent and they all sat down. Guy shrunk down in his seat and looked at me as if I'd lost my mind. The regular Israeli guy next to me on the other side nodded his head with raised eyebrows in Israeli-style approval. My heart was racing but missing that slot and staying on the plane with this lot simply wasn't an option. We made it home on time.

Next up for the senior team was Mike. There's quite a nice story with Mike. I was on another flight in a posh cabin for a holiday and this man stood next to my seat after take-off and said, "I'd recognise that voice anywhere." He was an old DJ client of mine and it turned out that when I had "retired" from social party work, I came out of retirement to do his fourth daughter in a row's Batmitzvah for which he was very grateful. He was a nice man called Tony, a very passionate Arsenal man and pretty big in property. He invited me down to his home on the beach for a 'natter'. I spent a few hours with him and he told me about his son-in-law, Mike, who he thought was doing good work for one of my competitors and was responsible for some great clients and maybe I should have a chat with him when back.

This was perfect for me: a younger guy, already with in's with clients, not getting enough from his bosses. I met with Mike and immediately offered him a job with share options. It took a bloody year to do that deal, but in the end, I got my man. Mike's biggest client was Jaguar Land Rover. I'd never done car work before and thought we could smash it with Mike reversing his cool car production work into our model. He wasn't sure as he had his own team, but in the end I convinced him and it turned out well for all of us. There were some potential legal issues with his old company, but I told Mike to just get on with it and I would deal with them.

Mike and Nicholas pitched for a major contract a few months later, and Mike specifically asked the client to make sure he didn't bump into his old company at the pitch. As he, Nicholas and Nikki waited in reception, Mike's old team walked out of their pitch. FUCK! I only heard about this the next day and then received a strongly worded legal letter from his former employers. I had promised him I would take care of it all and I kept my promise. I stuck the letter in my top drawer and ignored it. I ignored the next two letters as well and guess what? It went away… I knew they were on shaky ground and it would be expensive to sue, I wasn't prepared to spend money on lawyers. I never have been keen to do that, and for years, I had read my own contracts – they were often straightforward if not overly wordy, and I knew I wouldn't go to court and risk losing my company and spending 100s of thousands on lawyers for anything. My policy was simple: no lawyers for anything except *really* heavy staff issues or the sale of the business. Mike also slowly bought into the business along with Guy, and I now had three partners.

An arena we had always been involved in and created for was TV; TV was Nicholas's background and we all decided to hire a Head of TV and potentially expand. Steve Carsey was and still is the best writer of a document I have ever known; fucking hell, he could write brilliant emails and he was brimming with TV ideas. He was behind the smash hit *Robot Wars* and whilst we had made loads of TV, we had never had a smash hit. The right idea can go global and despite lots of bad experiences with TV, the company was flying and I thought we should capitalise and go for more TV again. I was doubling down as I had just had the most awful television experience imaginable. It annoys me even writing it down for this book, but here goes....

Before Steve, our quasi-Head of TV was the very lovely Bob Massie. Bob was steeped in television, he had worked for ITV for many years and knew Nicholas of old from the *Big Breakfast*. I just offered Bob an office and a desk and said we could do co-productions if the right thing came along.

One day, my friend Martin (Atomic Kitten's manager from Liverpool) wanted me to meet the recent winner of *Big Brother*, an Essex lad called Brian Bellow; Martin told me he had a TV idea. Brian came in to see me and told me about all his mates in Essex. He explained that there was a TV show in America on MTV called *The Hills*, it was a constructed reality concept based around some young characters in Beverly Hills. I had vaguely heard of it. Brian said he thought this bunch he was connected with were real characters; he told me about Mark Wright, Amy Childs, Kirk Norcross and a few others. It sounded mad, and in my view, brilliant. I immediately called Bob in and told Brian to tell Bob what he had just told me. Bob exclaimed, "If this is all true, then it's gold!" I'll never forget that moment. I asked Bob what we needed to do and he told me we needed to go to

Essex and film a sizzle, like a teaser of what the show could be. We came up with the title *Totally Essex* and I paid for the production of the sizzle, which was indeed "gold". These characters were brilliant. The accents, the attitudes, the looks, everything was just as Brian had said. OMG, I thought, we've finally done it, we've found the 'golden TV goose'.

Bob then set about trying to sell the concept to ITV and others. I'm not going to make this story longer than it needs to be, because it still annoys me. Essentially ITV and Lime Pictures STOLE our idea and if you are reading this and disagree then fucking sue me, you cunts! All the original stars of *The Only Way is Essex* have written in their books about how it all began. Bob and Brian had spent months trying to make it happen and the very people they pitched to stole the idea. I was done with TV, it had no scruples, it was a horrible business and I wanted out. That sizzle only cost me about £15k, it was a cheap lesson, but Bob and Brian were crushed. They wanted to sue, but I didn't want to go to court over anything and told them so. In the next year, with my unknowing help, they found a pretty shady lawyer who offered them a no-win, no-fee deal and they slowly pursued their case. I asked them to keep me out of it as I viewed it as negative energy and I had a business to run and didn't need the distraction. About one year later, the case was about to go to court and they all begged me to add Sassy's name to the petition. I reluctantly agreed as I felt bad for both Bob and Brian. *TOWIE* had become a big hit show. We had all missed out on a life-changing opportunity due to at best 'bad practise' and at worst downright theft. Somebody sent me a video of a TV conference in Edinburgh with the main *TOWIE* production team being interviewed on stage. Kate Garraway asked the panel who had come up with the name. One of the producers said, "Well, it was called *Totally Essex* at first, but I can't remember who changed it." That was absolute proof in my mind, so I said they could use our name in the case.

It was all simply wrong; people were making millions out of this genre by now and we had zip, fuck all. As the court date approached, they tried to do a deal and I always said no. This was potentially many, many millions of pounds, "You've come this far, let's go to court," and then I went on holiday to our home in Florida. Nicholas, my partner, went to court with Brian and Bob – I just didn't want to – and then the barristers, Queen's Council and lawyers, in my view, ganged up on Brian, Bob and Nicholas. They told them they had been offered £1m to settle and that we should accept as we had no chance of actually winning. About 9am in Florida, Nicholas called me and said Brian and Bob wanted the money and he felt, as he had been advised that we would not win, that he had no option but to accept. "Please tell me you didn't settle," I enquired. He felt he had no choice; I got it, but I was pissed off and went to play golf and forget about the whole thing. It was intrinsically wrong, they had gotten away with theft and £1m was nothing compared to what they would earn from this franchise. Cunts!

When I returned from holiday, I asked Nick what we would net from this. He told me to sit down. The lawyers' fees were apparently over £800,000. What?? How could they be, they'd only really been working on this for a few weeks leading up to the court date. Brian and Bob shared about £165k and we got £35k. The fucking lawyers were bent too!! Jesus!! The lawyers' firm then went after me for all the VAT as none of the others were registered for VAT – it would have resulted in me making a substantial cash loss on everything after 'winning'. I point-blank refused and they kept pursuing me for months which would have been quite scary as they were lawyers, but I was incandescent with rage. I'd already been ripped off once, fuck 'em. A few years later, I noticed that the lead lawyer got fired from his firm. I should have stuck to my guns – never go to court for anything – if you are going to be diddled in life, just dust yourself down and get on with positive energy stuff; if you surround yourself with negativity, it will take you down. Never again.

Steve was now our new Head of TV and he really tried hard to make things happen, and despite being bitten by the Essex thing, I thought he could do it. I was sad when we realised that it wasn't going to happen, at least not on a timescale that was economically viable. We gave it a year, maybe that wasn't long enough, and we parted ways, nicely. Steve went on to run original content at Audible and they became a huge client of Sassy's. I always appreciated Steve's wisdom and it was a shame we couldn't make TV work as Nicholas and I had done well in the early years, but enough was enough.

Chapter 27

Kids

Robbie & Kylie

M y ex-wife, Belinda, and I have three great children – Joe, Louis and Saskia – and what amazes me today is how different they all are. They each have attributes from both parents, good and bad. For any new parents reading this, I maintain you do not fall head over heels in love with your child from the moment they are born, they are just a bundle of screaming little limbs with no personality and they are practically blind. I imagine it could be different for mums, they have nurtured them for nine months and there could be an instant connection.

As babies, they were all different – Joe wouldn't eat and spent most of the time dribbling, Louis wouldn't stop crying and Saskia was an angel. Then they grew up… Honestly, they were all good kids, but I think I was pretty strict and maybe they didn't have a choice. Our friends bought their children up with less discipline and all I'll say is, "I'm happy with mine." I love theirs but I'm happy with mine.

One night, our friends the Dryan's couldn't get their fourth child, Harry, to sleep. He was a little bugger in those days, he just wouldn't go to sleep and would cry incessantly. We were over with a small crowd of friends listening on the baby monitor to this incessant crying. I asked if I could have a go. "Knock yourself out," replied Drysie, and up I went. Harry was standing up in his cot bawling his eyes out. "Lie down," I ordered in a very terse, deep voice. "Lie down and shut the fuck up, do you hear me, you little fucker? Shut up!" He was about eight months old. He laid down with his eyes wide open, staring in horror at me. "Shut your eyes, now," I commanded very strongly. I had completely forgotten about the baby monitor and came back down to about ten friends all crowded around it in shocked silence. He slept very well thereafter.

Belinda and I were virtually always on the same page when it came to the kids' upbringing. If one felt some discipline or loving was required then it was dispensed by both of us. I truly believe that's all you need, plenty of love and discipline.

They all have different personalities: Joe is so like me it's scary, very sure of himself, kind, reserved (not like me) and has an ambitious desire to achieve. He is so popular amongst his friends and doesn't like to spread himself too thinly when it comes to friendship; just like me, his friends have been with him since school and earlier. I think Joe is at his best one-on-one or two-on-two, now with his lovely wife and my daughter-in-law, Tamara. He will be a great husband and dad. By the time you read this, he will have a daughter and me a granddaughter. Joe works in financial technology and is doing great.

Louis is a lovely boy, one of the most popular I know. People are always telling me how lovely he is and, quite fantastically, he always laughs at my jokes. Louis came on board at Sassy Films at the age of 18 and that wasn't easy for him. We were both a bit nervous about him being in 'daddy's business', but in the end, it's what he wanted and I thought we had such a great broad stroke over the production world that he would learn well there. I didn't go easy on him, probably the opposite. He has now been there over ten years, he's a senior producer and a bloody good one. His laid-back attitude belies his desire to do well. I recently found the cutest school essay he wrote aged about 11 where he stated he wanted to be 'a TV producer like my Dad', brilliant. He is and I couldn't be prouder. Louis is a sensitive soul and has a lot of love to give the right girl when she comes along (maybe she just did!).

Saskia – Oy! Where do I begin? As I have mentioned, we are convinced she was one of two; she was different to the boys and her friends, she was shy (not now), quiet (not now), had few opinions (not now)... the list goes on. Thinking about it today, despite being the apple of our eyes, it wasn't easy for Sassy (only I'm allowed to call her that apparently). She's four years younger than her brothers and whilst they were off doing what boys do, she couldn't as she was too young. She was soooo cute though. The boys were probably a bit mean to her growing up, but never meaning to be hurtful. They just treated her like they treated each other, not allowing much for the difference in age or sex. I didn't really understand or know how isolated Saskia felt at times during her childhood, she only let me know in her early twenties. Joe and Louis always shared a room, they had each other as they were only 13 months apart which I think was tough for Saskia.

As Rod Stewart sang, *I wish that I knew what I know now, when I was younger* – I think that's my favourite lyric ever. It makes me sad that in those young, formative years she felt that she didn't really have a voice in our busy family dynamic. She has certainly made up for it now as a journalist who graduated with a First-Class Honours degree from Edinburgh University. I also didn't realise how close we were until Belinda and I split. Looking back at photos, she was always in my arms and today I love being her dad as I do my boys' too.

I am delighted that today they are all close and when they need to they rally together. Sassy marks her space, and she and Joe have intelligent conversations; I think they quietly respect each other. Louis cares but in his own laid-back style. He was best man at Joe's wedding and will always help Saskia even if he can't help the odd, "I just don't get you" comment. I have a picture that was taken in LA at my brother's 50th which for me sums up all of their personalities precisely as I have described. It's going to be on the wall in the Cotswolds home I am building. I am so proud of all three of them as they begin their journeys into adulthood… I am positive they will all get what they want out of life, positive!

Chapter 28

A Reason to Believe

Rod Stewart

I was never really sure if I was going to write this chapter. You'll have to read the lyrics or listen to the song to get the line that made me title this chapter with this classic.

When I met Belinda, I was 25; she was the first girl I could stand for more than a week. From the very beginning, we didn't part and we fell in love. I always felt our marriage was very strong – we were a good team, but perhaps over time something shifted. Once kids have grown up and nearly gone from the family home, it's a tumultuous time for any mother, particularly one who has been focused on bringing up children for over 20 years. There were times in our marriage where I felt we were 100%, particularly during a period when Belinda studied to be a marriage guidance councillor. She had real purpose, she studied hard and took it seriously and we were able to come together in the evenings and share – we were both doing worthwhile stuff. Sadly, she gave the work up soon after qualifying, stating that she would be spending too much time in America at our second home, and that wouldn't work for her clients.

A few years later, with the kids going off to uni and starting work, I felt she had lost any sense of purpose; those are my feelings and I know I am not speaking on her behalf. In 2015, I felt something was up, behaviour patterns weren't the same. I couldn't put my finger on it, but something was definitely up. When we split, I found a clip from Will Smith saying how couples shouldn't rely on each other for happiness. I agree. I was fulfilled – I had my work, my friends, football, golf, poker and coming together at the end of the day, it felt like the conversations were one-way traffic. I'll never forget being told to stop talking about my work, that it was boring… I was put out, but I stopped.

The simple truth is that we grew apart; it's a cliché, but it's true. Belinda did have a dalliance but that wasn't the reason we split. It was an easy excuse, but the truth was that we drifted. I felt she was unnecessarily sour towards me and she probably felt that she was no longer my priority. We did try hard, including couple's counselling after the "affair", but after a particularly rough period, I had to leave. For me, the fun, tipsy girl at parties wasn't so fun on the way home… Lots of people in our circle knew what I seemingly didn't; they knew she was not happy and consequently mean to me when I just thought it was part of our schtick.

Upon reflection, we had a great marriage until it wasn't great. I have no regrets of our time together and only wish her well today. During our divorce, I felt I was decent and fair, she got half of everything (and some) and even a top-up when I sold Sassy three years after we split. Without Belinda's support, I wouldn't have been successful; she typed up that first business plan that I showed Julian and always had faith in me. I hope we can become good friends again as our children have children.

I left the marriage and I was very sad. I moved into a tiny shoebox of a flat opposite Mill Hill Broadway station. I had gotten to the point where the loss of material things like my cinema room, poker room and an amazing flat that we had moved into just didn't matter as much as I had told myself they did. I had no idea how things would pan out, and I didn't know if friends would side with Belinda or me, or remain neutral. When I started to tell people about us splitting, they were floored, they couldn't believe it, except several close friends and even some family who knew more than I did. I had 'bitten my lip' for three years, clinging on to the hope that we could keep everything together. I desperately wanted Saskia to go to university and wouldn't jeopardise that for anything. Parents splitting is hard enough but when you have exams to do it could have been a disaster.

At work, I felt I had to tell my business partners; they were shocked but supportive as I explained that I might be a bit distracted for a while. They wished me well and we simply carried on. I hadn't been single for 28 years, my last experience of being single was as a young 20-something; maybe I would pick up where I left off? People told me there were lots of women out there and I was somewhat eligible. Realistically, that was never going to happen. I wasn't about to go out 'on the pull' aged 53, and the thought of online dating freaked me out. I had no idea and no intention of even looking. I first had to get my head straight and learn how to enjoy my own company.

Chapter 29

Keep on Moving

Soul II Soul

We were continuing to build the business and we were doing well. We had crazy live TV ads to produce, one of which, believe it or not was for the charity Cancer Research and the live commercial went out on Channel 4 INSIDE a human body. It was a live on air colonoscopy. I declined to direct this one.

I loved filming concerts and by now had shot hundreds of great acts for television or home video/ DVD, but those markets were all but gone. Then one day, a nice man called Philip Solomons came to see me about shooting gigs for cinemas. We knew how to shoot and broadcast live via satellite into cinemas because of our work doing the premieres. I loved this idea and we managed to land Take That, which ended up being a big box-office hit. We went on to do the next two tours with Take That, and three Cliff Richard and Westlife shows, and they all did great. We had found a new route to market for rock and pop shows and were among the first in the world to take this sector where it deserved to be. Long before the Beyoncés and Taylor Swifts had monster concert film hits.

I remember filming a fabulous Culture Club show for my brother who was now managing them. It was going to be in front of an audience but a second wave of Covid put paid to that. I ended up producing the whole show, booking Wembley Arena and everything to do with the staging. My favourite bit was PK walking in and seeing what we had done and him just saying it was "world class, Stevie, world class." That made me happy as he can be a tricky customer, but we really did smash it.

I knew that one day I wanted to sell Sassy films; I had been doing it for a long time and took my responsibilities very seriously. I had three partners, surely now I could pick and choose what jobs I wanted to do… yes, I could, and that's where the problems started for me. I began to take my foot off the pedal so to speak. After 30 plus years, couldn't the others sweat a bit too? I wasn't tired, maybe just a little bored.

I started making my Rock 'n' Roll Neons around this time. I'm really proud of them and the overall concept. I'd collate albums of my favourite artists, those that had made enough of them to allow me to create the montage. I'd handwrite a suitable defining lyric out, then have it blown into real neon glass in order to create the artwork. They are great and I've been commissioned a few times by some of my acquaintances to create a few more. The collection of Bowie, U2, Bruce Springsteen, Duran Duran, Michael Jackson, Prince, The Beatles and more are still for sale (see stevekemsley.com).

Back to Sassy films; don't get me wrong, if the job offered creative excitement I wanted in. My partners were bringing in higher budget jobs, jobs that required a lot of brown-nosing, justifying, long documents, briefing meetings and the dreaded director's treatment. I wasn't interested in all that stuff. My entire career, I had won work on passion and promise; maybe times were changing, but my co-workers were increasingly unwilling to put me in front of these new clients like big car manufacturers and

Amazon. I've never liked doing treatments, they trap you to a creative that could still be evolving. Whenever I had storyboards to shoot, I was committed to just shooting the boards. That's when you cover just the pre-agreed shots, boring!!!

I remember producing and directing a great music video for The Kingdom Choir called Blinded By Your Grace. I loved that job, along with a couple of secret camera set-ups for Soda Stream featuring the world's strongest man dressed up as Santa, and my favourite was for a new digital bank called Tandem. It took the piss out of the traditional banking service with a secret camera set up in a pub where the bartender pressed a cassette player with hold music when someone ordered a pint. It's on YouTube; check it out.

I love the music and the funny stuff. In the early days, Nikki would write the scripts, then I would make changes, she'd produce and I would direct. It was fun changing shots around on the day and having the freedom to think on your feet. She would get a little frustrated but that work was always approved and always successful. It felt different now. Nikki was working with Guy more on the client-facing stuff and I was seemingly left to do HR stuff and only got to shoot if I really insisted, like a cool Jaguar shoot in

New York with the star of Baby Driver – Ansel Elgort, which I only produced as my good friend, Brian Klein, the famous director of Top Gear, had the car creds that the client needed to protect their mortgage payments. Luckily, I got on so well with BK that both the trip and shoot were good fun. Brian and I have been close for many years, but in the early days of video, we were absolute rivals. Between the two of us, we produced nearly all the video industry's sell-through output. Not bad for a couple of Jew boys from London. We became friendly later, but our work swords crossed many times.

I had produced the TV ad for Jeremy Clarkson's first-ever home video. The ad went down in legend, I mentioned it earlier, but because Brian knew Jeremy well, he picked up his production work thereafter and made a fucking fortune from it. You're welcome, BK. Once we were both after the same Geri Halliwell Yoga video work; I didn't know Brian was charged with trying to sign her as well. They said absolutely no to both of us, but as I have said previously, my tenacity won out in that instance.

So here I was finding myself not inspired to shoot on a daily basis and feeling left out. I know, I thought, I'll sell the business to my partners, then came Covid!

My marriage was over, I was living in a small flat in Mill Hill and we were locked down.

By now, I had reacquainted myself with my old bank manager, Sasha. I was sitting at my desk one day and one of those LinkedIn updates dropped into my inbox. I hadn't lived with Belinda for about ten months by now; I clicked on the link and saw it was Sasha. We had always stayed in touch, she was such a brilliant bank manager. We probably spoke once a year sort of thing and maybe had lunch once every couple of years. She had remained in finance and kept connected with many of her old clients. We were friends, she knew about my financial life and always had a wise word to share. I swear I never thought of her in any other way than a good professional contact. We occasionally chatted about our lives as she was a million miles from mine and I hers. Anyway, this LinkedIn update was a new picture of her. Blimey, I thought, she never used to look like that, did she? It turned out she had been in New York with girlfriends and had just had a Charlotte Tilbury makeover. Her picture was strikingly attractive. Without hesitating, I grabbed my phone and dialled her number.

We met for a drink a few weeks later, which was nothing unusual. She tells me I was a bit sad as I told her my story. She began wondering if it was too early for her to tell me that she'd always had a soft spot for me. I didn't spot it. A month or so later, we arranged a lunch. I had started to think about her in a different way and the lunch was mildly flirty. I dropped her at the station, we kissed goodbye, kind of on the lips. OMG! This was the first woman I had kissed on the lips in 28 years (other than my wife)! She waltzed off to catch her train back to Cheltenham where she lived, and I was spinning.

We started seeing each other very quietly at first. I didn't want anyone to know, even though it had been a year since Belinda and I had split; I needed privacy to know where this would leave me feeling. During our first night together, we went to dinner and held hands whilst we walked to the restaurant. OMG! This was also only the second woman I had held hands with in 28 years. It freaked me out… I found these early experiences really weird and had a proper wobble but we survived and are very happily together as I write this some five years later.

Sasha is just perfect for me. She says things like, "Try and say the second thing that comes into your head"; such good advice that I really ought to try more often.

There is one crazy story involving me and Sasha; long after my divorce and after lockdown which was largely spent at Sasha's in Cheltenham, where long Cotswold walks ensued, I decided that after selling our American home I still missed the second home life... Boca had been my happy place and I needed to find another happy place. My flat in Mill Hill was ok but it was a real step down from my previous life as I was now worth half what I had before the divorce. I still had a big mortgage and was all but going to have to start the business afresh after Covid. The Cotswolds, I was discovering, was beautiful and wouldn't cost two Club Class tickets to Miami to get to. Why didn't we find a house together out here I suggested. We started looking at small cottages, we spent the best part of a year driving around northern Cotswolds looking and dreaming about what our dream house and future might look like. We were good together.

Slowly but surely, my kids met Sasha. I knew after a few weeks that I was done. I'd found someone I was happy to stay with, first time out. I felt incredibly fortunate and still can't quite believe how lucky we both are to have found each other after we both went through some pretty rough times respectively. Back to the story... we couldn't find anywhere, so we decided to look online for a shit-hole with a view. Both of us had experience doing up houses and thought we could do it one more time in order to build a home together. A few months later, she found it: a shit-hole with a view. I offered the asking price on the spot when I went back to see it and the offer was accepted. There was one problem though. I didn't have any money. I decided I would sell my office building that I had kept in the divorce and put the money into more bricks and mortar, but this time, build the house of our dreams. That was the idea, but when I made and had the offer accepted, it was just an idea. I called a good friend and asked if I could borrow the money; without hesitating, they said yes. I then explained how I was going to pay them back and that I would pay interest, but they explained that they had already said yes. That phone call took two minutes or was it 30 years to build up that sort of trust? We bought the house and then went about designing it ourselves… during this entire process, we discovered we had such similar tastes, which was a joy.

Here's the kicker – I eventually sold the building and with the money began to create our dream home. Do you remember who'd lent me the money earlier to buy the building I had just sold? Sasha Speed! Turns out she made a good decision to lend me that money 18 years earlier. The house isn't finished as I type this, but it's getting there, and upon clearing out some old files, I found the loan agreement that Sasha as my bank manager and I signed in 2006. The signature page is going on the downstairs loo wall in our new home!

Back to Sassy films, I wasn't happy and, as I mentioned, I wanted to sell; I wanted out. I was being left out – I felt isolated by my partners and even senior staff. The business had changed drastically during Covid, or maybe I had.

Chapter 30

Pride

Spandau Ballet

We all remember how sunny it was during that first lockdown, but before I could enjoy any sunshine, I had to look at Sassy Films and see if we could save the company. We waited three months but in months two and three, business went to virtually zero and our overheads were killing us. Another two months like that and we would have been insolvent; that was very clear. I wanted to stay with Sasha rather than sit in my flat alone so my 'bubble' went to Cheltenham. Just before full lockdown, there was something I had to do and it was the most difficult conversation I had ever had in my life.

Nicholas had been my partner for 18 years and his side of the business was now totally dead. He sat across all the live work we did but there was a problem. For the past two years, Nicholas had been distracted. I don't know all the details as to why and it's not my story to tell but he wasn't really 'in the room'. He came in every day, stuck his headphones on and we never saw or heard from him. I'll never forget going into his office to talk and explain that because of the precarious financial position we were in, he had to go. He was being paid the same as me and the business just couldn't afford it. I've never been so nervous, ever. I loved Nick; he was my friend and partner and he wasn't the only one who would be affected.

We all had to take a minimum of 60% pay cuts. The government furlough scheme was a godsend, but it didn't save many jobs, and I hurt a lot of people with decisions that we had to make, for which I am truly sorry. I had to lead this push and was very fair to all financially but that didn't stop the pain. We bought Nicholas's shares from him and paid him very fairly. Despite the hurt, Nick and I have remained friends and have been chatting recently about future opportunities. When I came to sell the business in 2023, I visited Nicholas and gave him more money. Contractually, I didn't have to, but he was there for me when we were good and I know he was grateful for that last cheque!

Writing this makes me feel a little sick; it was an awful time but I still feel today that I had no choice. A few former senior staff members don't talk to me now because of this period, which makes me sad, but I hope the vast majority whose jobs were saved by our measures are grateful. Guy and I sat down and worked on spreadsheets over Zooms, we got £500,000 loan from our bank and somehow survived. This was probably the toughest period of my working life. The crash in 2008 wobbled me personally and mentally but actually we were ok; this time, we were not ok, but thankfully I was. It was a battle and I was going through a divorce at the same time!

I had waited patiently to get divorced and I think we both thought it was a good idea to get it sorted before Joe, our eldest, married Tamara. We did it without expensive lawyers, although Belinda had assistance from a well-meaning friend. I found the process utterly exhausting and ended up giving Belinda security and over half of our estate with monthly payments going too far into the future, but honestly, they wore me down. I was happy with Sasha, and I just wanted it done. Today, upon reflection, I would have done the same, save one major detail which ended up biting me squarely on the arse, but hey ho, best I keep it private as opinions will differ.

Writing all this down now shows me how much trauma there was in my life during those Covid years. On top of all that, my Dad got taken ill. Mum called me one day, as he had ended up on the bathroom floor and she couldn't get him up. He hadn't been feeling well but didn't want to go to hospital and get Covid, such was the fear the government spread. It turned out he had a nasty kidney infection and simply had to succumb to hospitalisation bang in the middle of lockdown. He duly contracted Covid as well whilst in hospital and it was an extremely worrying time; he saw several people die on that Covid ward, but he survived, and as I write, he is 86 and doing really well. Mum recently celebrated her 80th birthday surrounded by many grandchildren, which I know made her happy. I am blessed not to have had tragic losses in my life and reflecting on this makes the shit Covid years seem not that disastrous. We got through it, many didn't, we got away with it. "That, which doesn't kill you"… as I've said is a mantra I stand by. The most unpleasant mantra that I don't live by but always seems to be true is, "No good deed goes unpunished" – it's a shame but, in my experience, bloody true, most of the time… I guess it all evens out in the end.

After Covid, I was feeling the same about work. I can

say that, despite owning the majority of shares in my business, I was feeling marginalised. I don't think I can blame anyone in particular, but it's the way it was, so I decided to turn this feeling into a strategy. I thought that if I did the least work and got paid the most money, my partners would start to feel resentful and maybe buy me out. I didn't think there was any other way, our numbers weren't great but ok. I came up with schemes and all three partners talked; we talked for nearly two years, but essentially we were just too far way on those numbers and ultimately decided to put our shoulders to the wheel and carry on… we just couldn't agree what Sassy Films was worth, even though I was prepared to be paid over a long interest-free period.

Then, literally, the day after we gave up on negotiations, an email landed in my inbox from a company who said they were interested in buying the company. I'm not going to bore you with the story as it's a corporate thing but within six months I sold all my shares (for what I always said they were worth) and my partners carried on. I know this is a brief summary, but it's really not that interesting. I got some dough which meant we could finish building the dream home in The Cotswolds, I could have some time to write this book and then go on to try and write a screenplay and finally make a movie (maybe)... many of you know what movie I wanna make and if you don't, you will soon.

Chapter 31

Straight Down The Middle

Bing Crosby

G olf has been a massive part of my life since Dad got me those lessons with Mark Tibbles. I've been great, just ok or really bad. My current handicap is 13.4 and can do everything well except chip, they call it 'the yips'... it's lasted ten years so far!

I took nine years away from golf when all the kids were little; it didn't seem fair to be working as hard as I was and then spending five to six hours playing golf on the weekend. Otherwise, I have played since I was young. I'm part of a fantastic golf society called WAGOS. It stands for "we've all got our stories". Any golfer will tell you a story as to why the didn't get a lower score or how many putts lipped out... the point is, it's boring and no one wants to hear it. We have a

WhatsApp group and the banter is hardcore, bordering on cruel, and when Arsenal play Spurs, I have to mute it. I have made so many great friends through golf and had the very best of times 'on tour'. My golf friends are entirely separate from any friends I have mentioned previously. I don't mix them with my regular life, they are unique, and frankly my other friends would struggle to understand all of them.

I have been lucky enough to play golf all over the world and I have a display of golf balls on the wall in my London flat with the top 50 courses I have played – it continues to be updated. The weird thing is, in our memories, we really enjoyed the courses we played the best on. I won't bore you with all 50, but my top five are: Royal County Down in Northern Ireland, Augusta, Kings Barns, St Andrews and Pebble Beach. Playing Scotland is the best of the best and I have been lucky enough to play a lot in America. At my golf club in Boca Raton, Florida, my regular game was Stevie A, Simon and Jason. Steve is one of my best mates and extremely successful. He has taken me all over and a particular favourite of ours were our trips the Vegas to play Shadow Creek and a bit of poker.

Going to Augusta is a dream for every and any golfer. My brother was friendly with a big-time insurance broker in New York; he, in turn, knew a member of the most famous golf club in golf history. Once a year, as a kindness, this member would offer his good friend a four-ball. You can't play at Augusta without a member, end of story. Legend has it that movie stars and presidents have been told no. As a 50th birthday present, PK got Stevie A a game at the hallowed course in Georgia and Stevie A, in turn, asked me. The two of us met at Atlanta airport, as I had a meeting at the head office of the Cabbage Patch Dolls emporium (for a tv ad job). When we drove up to the gates, we explained three times that we were guests and were told to meet at the club, we were staying on-site in one of the famous cabins, the one Rory hit when he blew his lead on the eleventh in 2014. The security guard was having none of it, until we mentioned the member's name, then he just said, "There you go" and opened the gates to Magnolia Lane... driving up that lane is something else for a golf fan. We met the member, who had to wear his green jacket for dinner, that night and proceeded to have the most unimaginably extraordinary two days. We played the main course two and a half times (the back nine was the extra half) and we played the par 3 course. We were not allowed to put our hands in our pockets, not even to tip the caddies. I told my caddy his tip depended on how many photos he took and not on his golfing advice; I got both and managed to drop a couple of $100 bills on the ground by my bag on our last nine without our host noticing. I even played well, admittedly we were off the front of each tee, but I shot 83 on one round and was buzzing. We were the only people there – imagine that, the entire estate to ourselves. I did my brains in the pro shop and spent too much.

At breakfast the following morning, a large African American waiter, resplendent in his white short jacket and black tie, rebuked me when I asked for a menu. "You can have whatever you want, sir," he explained… We were taken on a tour of the clubhouse, we saw the famous 'eagles nest', the wine cellars, Eisenhower's desk and of course the world-famous Augusta Masters trophy..it's a trip neither of us will ever forget for the rest of our lives.

Poker is another passion. I have two regular schools, my Friday Night game, which I only joined after my marriage broke down; Stevie A probably invited me out of pity and I love it. We play seven-card stud and the others are all a bit older than me. Many friends call me a bit of an 'old woman', you wanna meet this lot! I have played in my Monday Night game for over two decades with old and very good friends. We absolutely play for money and we can lose or win a few hundred quid at any given game, but the truth is that throughout the year, the money just goes around the table, except for the Big Dick – he loses nine out of ten.

Another favourite pastime is skiing. I started really quite late in life after that accident when I was on a school ski trip in Italy. I was 30 when I learnt with my friend Jason, he had such a spectacular accident a few years later he never went again and still has a disgusting protruding collar bone.

When he first made money, my bro took us skiing to Colorado; to this day it was the most expensive 'free' holiday I've ever had! The air was so thin it was difficult to catch your breath, particularly at -16 degrees. However, one of the best ten minutes of my life was on fresh powder there… it was so cold that the snow just evaporated like dust as my instructor and I blitzed through it. I remember Belinda not being too impressed when I described it as the best day of my life when I returned. We took the kids skiing when they were really young and they still expect to be taken as grown-ups. It's a bloody expensive holiday, especially when there are up to eight of us and I'm expected to fork out… but we all love it and I was thrilled when Sasha turned out to be a good skier too.

Back to the golf. My physical health isn't the best: I have had operations on my knee, my shoulders, a hernia or two, my feet ain't great and don't get me started on my back! I am constantly inspired to get better just so I can carry on playing. For my 50th birthday, I took some of my golf friends and family to Gleneagles and such is the infamy of my physical health that my best mates bought me a golf buggy! What a gift, thank you all!

Golf is the gift that keeps giving. It's crazy frustrating but we all play for those few fantastics shots that keep us out there. I hope I'm still at it when I'm 90!

Chapter 32

Friends

Shalamar

I'm blessed to say that I have strong, solid relationships with my brother, Mum and Dad and my kids and, together with my friends, they are my backbone. During all my tough times they were all there for me. When I got divorced I was worried our friends would split but they didn't. I am still friendly with everyone I have been friendly with for the past 30–40 years. Even some of Belinda's closest pals are amongst mine too.

PK and I share great friends, I love his and he loves mine. I can't name them all and they will be disappointed to think that they weren't worth a mention which of course is not true. I decided to keep my memoirs about stories and life lessons and just because you weren't involved in a remarkable event or life lesson doesn't mean we aren't as close as we are… I have some sensitive friends which is not easy as I can be a bit blunt, but for some reason they love me as I love them. Thank you to every single one of you , you know who you are. In a year or so, I'll have a 60th birthday celebration and those of you invited will know that it's you I'm talking about.

The last 'best' friend that slipped into my life much later than childhood was Tony Gibber. We just hit it off straight away. Tony is a music man although he is really a greengrocer… he composed so much wonderfully shit music for me in my home video days and we became really close. We would share divorce stories, advice, business concerns and have long chats. Tony hasn't been well of late so I wanted to commit my love for him to print.

The rest of you can fuck off – yes you, Stevie A, who I have shared more hours with than anyone thanks to playing golf all over the world. Giles, my builder, flatmate and friend in need it turned out. The Dryan family are one of our closest family friends, a family where I feel like a dad to those kids, despite the fact they have a very fine one of their own, who happens to be one of my best mates, Drysie (Simon). Roger and Lucy, Leanne and Brad, Nicola and Steven, my Cotswolds buddies, Michaela and Andrew. The Leslie twins. My mate Aly Hills who now lives in Australia. The Bergs. The Posners, who always offer us refuge in Antibes and are confidants extraordinaire. Julian will always be my 'partner'. There are so many more and I simply can't mention them all here. There are stories for each and every one of you. You've lent me houses, cars, money, your time, your hysteria. We've seen our kids grow and become friendly, we've laid people to rest and seen grandchildren born. Thank you all for being a friend – without you all, I couldn't and wouldn't be me.

I have had so many work colleagues over nearly 40 years but I have to single out Nikki and Harsha; they both joined me in the early days of Banana then came over to Sassy, working with me for over 22 and 25 years respectively, and I worked very closely with both of them. They are resolutely loyal and 'get me'. I will always be grateful to them both for the years we worked together, building two businesses. Nikki, my partner in crime on the production and creative front, and Harsha for running our accounts. Ladies, I will always be in your corner should you ever need me as you were in mine for most of our working lives. I also have to mention the late great Marshall Venier.

Marshy passed away in 2021. I have employed people for over 30 years, probably over 200 and I have never met anyone like Marshall. No member of staff ever told me they loved me after a brief normal meeting. Marshall was literally one of the nicest human beings I've ever encountered in my life, we spent hours together shooting toy ads and all sorts, he was a joy and an inspiration to me and everyone that worked with him.

Lastly, thank you to my best friend Sasha.

I love you all, every which way, very much.

Chapter 33

My Favourite Things

The Supremes

Albums:

North of a Miracle – Nick Heyward
Live & Dangerous – Thin Lizzy
Pelican West – Haircut 100
The River – Bruce Springsteen
Songs in the Key of Life – Stevie Wonder
Breakfast in America – Supertramp
Lexicon of Love – ABC
LA is My Lady – Frank Sinatra
Punch the Clock – Elvis Costello
Jarreau – Al Jarreau
Eat to the Beat – Blondie
Christopher Cross – Christopher Cross

Singers:

George Michael
Rod Stewart
Jamie Cullum
Bono
Freddie Mercury
Barry Manilow
Karen Carpenter
Elvis
Frank Sinatra
Michael Bublé
Luther Vandross
Amy Winehouse

Songwriters:

Lennon & McCartney
Nick Heyward
George Michael
Mick & Keith
Billy Joel
Stevie Wonder
Bruce Springsteen
Tim Rice-Oxley
Prince
David Bowie
Elton & Bernie
Sting

Bands:

Rolling Stones
Keane
U2
Haircut 100
Beatles
Thin Lizzy
Culture Club
Duran Duran
INXS
Oasis
Supertramp
Spandau Ballet

Gigs:

Live Aid 1 – Wembley Stadium
U2 at The Sphere – Las Vegas
Prince – Love Sexy – Wembley Arena
Queen – Wembley stadium
Simply Red – The Forum Kentish Town
Roachford – The Forum Kentish Town
Take That – O2 Arena
Rolling Stones – Spielberg – Austria
Stevie Wonder – Louisville – Kentucky
Culture Club – Hammersmith Ocean
Wham! The Final (warm up) Brixton Acadamy
Wild Horses – Marquee Club – Wardour Street
Bruno Mars – Mexico

Movies:

Les Misérables
Oliver!
Fiddler on the Roof
Schindler's List
Secrets & Lies
Gangs of New York
Rain Man
Dances with Wolves
La La Land
Zone of Interest
Crash
Whiplash

Golf Courses: (played)

Royal County Down
Augusta National
Pebble Beach
Kings Barns
St Andrews
Shadows Creek
Trump Aberdeen
Gullan
Bora
Nairn
Carnoustie
Sunningdale

~ END ~

Very special thanks to my fabulous editors, without your attention to detail, this book would read like the mad ramblings of a nut job – Nikki, Sasha & Lucy.

Taking my design and creating the sleeve – Bob.

Nat and Rachael at The Book Typesetters and for holding my debut publishing hand, the wonderful Amy Warren at The Writing House.